STUDENT-FRIENDLY GUIDES

Skilful time management!

D0140064

STUDENT-FRIENDLY GUIDES

Skilful time management!

PETER LEVIN

Open University Press

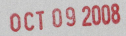

Open University Press
McGraw-Hill Education
McGraw-Hill House
Shoppenhangers Road
Maidenhead
Berkshire
England
SL6 2QL

email: enquiries@openup.co.uk
world wide web: www.openup.co.uk

and Two Penn Plaza, New York, NY 10121-2289, USA

First published 2007

A catalogue record of this book is available from the British Library

ISBN 13-978 0335 222 940 (pb)
     10-0335 222 943 (pb)

Library of Congress Cataloging-in-Publication Data
CIP data applied for

Typeset by YHT Ltd, London
Printed in the UK by Bell & Bain Ltd, Glasgow

Contents

The myth of 'time management'

READ THIS FIRST!

The term 'time management' is in common use. Type it into an internet search engine and you'll find millions of references to it. But take a moment to look at it literally and you'll see that it's a complete contradiction in terms: *time cannot be managed!* Time just keeps flowing steadily past you: 60 minutes per hour, 24 hours per day, 7 days per week. There is absolutely nothing you can do to manage this flow. You have to live with it.

If you can't manage time, what *can* you do with it? My answer is that you can make the most of it. You can work out what you want to do with it – your goals, what you want to achieve – and you can work out how best to create and organize the activities necessary to achieve those goals. In other words, you can work out how best to use time and manage *yourself*. The principle on which this book is based is that it is perfectly possible to manage yourself – your activities, the things you do, indeed your whole life – to make the most of the time that you have available. And my aim in writing this book is to help you to realize precisely that possibility.

Time plays a central part in your academic life. The academic cycle repeats year after year. During each term or semester you'll have a weekly teaching timetable, a kind of 'treadmill'. Exams at the end of the academic year or semester are held on set dates that constitute 'deadlines' for you, as do hand-in dates for essays, project reports and other coursework. You will need to organize your work – indeed your whole life – around these cycles and deadlines.

As you might expect from the number of web pages in existence, there is a lot of advice around on 'time management' for students. Your own university might well have produced its own: there's a kind of 'college industry' in existence, with every study skills centre and counselling service producing its own miscellaneous collection of homespun advice. I'm sure that much of this advice – if not all of it – is well intentioned, but some of the advice is a counsel of perfection: if you're sufficiently well organized to put it all into practice your 'time management' is probably pretty good already. Some of the advice is so abstract and unspecific that it doesn't help you work out what you should actually *do* ('Draw up a plan'; 'Always plan ahead'). And some of it is plain unrealistic for most people.

There are also some popular self-help books in print, dedicated to helping you use your time productively. While many of these have their enthusiastic devotees, they are mainly targeted at managers: people running large organizations, with projects to manage and staff to delegate to. Such books don't deal specifically with the very special culture and circumstances in which you, as a student, find yourself: the ethos of individual achievement coupled with being treated as one of a mass of students; the unquantifiable task of learning, of 'getting your head round stuff', which can easily take up all the hours of the day, and more, if you let it; being on the receiving end of deadlines superimposed on weekly, termly and academic yearly cycles; and so on.

In the context of 'time management', 'planning' means 'planning ahead'. Planning ahead to do a piece of work that involves learning is not easy, because everything you do when you're learning involves an element of novelty, of newness, and accordingly some uncertainty. You hardly ever have an exactly similar past experience to refer to, and you never know what tomorrow will bring: some new insight or piece of information may come your way that sets you off on a different track or sends you back to revise what you have spent the past three weeks writing.

And much of the advice on websites for students is not exactly helpful, to say the least. Certainly, general advice to 'plan ahead' ignores two facts: first, the fact that planning is effective only if it is part of a system of management that also incorporates provision for monitoring whether work is on track to attain planned objectives, and for taking corrective action if it is not; second, the fact that planning entails something more than just gauging what you will need to do to attain an objective and then saying that you are going to do it – it involves *committing yourself* to doing it. This creates a dilemma for everyone doing academic work, because on the one hand committing yourself involves 'fixing' the future, determining what will happen at future points in time, whereas on the other hand the uncertainty inherent in academic work requires you to be flexible, leaving the future open. This dilemma is one that every student has to face up to; your self-management system has to be able to handle it.

In the business of self-management for students there are no 'one size fits all' remedies. No prescription will suit everybody. So in this book I offer a range of down-to-earth strategies and techniques, to enable you to choose and use the ones that you find to be appropriate to you in the situation in which you find yourself. Throughout, the thought at the back of my mind is that as a student you may find it helpful to have some assistance with taking control of your life and pattern of work, rather than being buffeted and pressurized by the demands of your teachers and institution.

Taking control of your life and work will open up some possibilities for you. In particular, it should allow you to develop your own vision of what you want to get out of your time at university. It's very easy, especially if you're following a degree programme with a high level of 'continuous assessment', to become preoccupied with jumping through the hoops that the institution sets for you. And much of the advice given to students on 'time management' fosters the idea that your time is to be used on fulfilling these tasks.

Please, be your own person! Think about what, besides the qualification bestowed on you when you graduate, you would like to get out of the three or four or however many years you'll spend being a student. Set your own sights, think about what you want to learn, and you will undoubtedly get more out of university than if you just allow yourself to be 'processed'. If you don't want to emerge at the end like an item off a production line, please do think for yourself about the person you want to become, and devote some of your time to achieving that vision.

It's also the case, I believe, that the more you can take control of your life and work, the less unnecessary stress you will be under. If my experience is anything to go by, and you're like most students, you don't need to be stressed to make you work, and increasing the stress on you leads to poorer work, not better. Correspondingly, you should find that less stress will help you to produce better work, as well as greater enjoyment of your studies. In my book, this can only be a good thing.

If my conversations with hundreds of students on the subject of 'time management' have taught me anything, it is that actually having a conversation helps the two of us to establish a 'common reality', a shared understanding of the obstacles that are being experienced by the student in making best use of his or her time. This shared understanding then provides us with a basis for finding a way forward and surmounting those obstacles. In the course of our conversation it often happens that both of us reassess the assumptions and taken-for-granteds that we started off with. Writing a book and having it published is plainly very much a one-way mode of communicating: it's nothing like having a conversation, however much I try to put myself in the place of a reader. But I do reproduce in these pages many of the questions that students have put to me during my career as an adviser to students, along with the answers that they and I together have come up with.

Working with students has been a huge privilege for me. I am enormously grateful to have had the opportunity to enter into their worlds and contribute to their learning and problem-solving. Students who are faced with the confusing and often mystifying demands of the academic system are in a uniquely vulnerable position, yet they have, with very few exceptions, been open and frank with me about their difficulties – and generous with their appreciation of the help I have given them. I take this opportunity to acknowledge with heartfelt thanks their partnership in the production of this book.

Peter Levin

Introduction

In my one-to-one work with students, problems around the use of time crop up very frequently. I get told things like:

- I haven't got time to do all the reading I'm expected to do
- I keep putting work off to the very last minute
- I can never hand work in on time
- I'm a perfectionist, and I hate handing in work that I'm not satisfied with, so I don't
- My life seems to consist of crises; I'm always stumbling in a panic from one deadline crisis to the next
- I'm always staying up late to finish work, then I oversleep and miss lectures and classes the next day
- However much time I make available, the work always expands to more than fill it
- I keep setting myself deadlines – and then I can't keep to them!
- I feel guilty if I take a day off.

The good news is that it is almost always possible to find strategies and techniques for dealing with these problems. And that when they are dealt with, the result is better-quality work, higher marks and a happier person. These are essentially strategies for using your time: 'time-use strategies'. In Part One of this book I present the elementary theory behind creating and implementing time-use strategies. In Part Two I address the many 'How to ...' issues that students face in making use of their time, and I suggest strategies and techniques for resolving these issues. All these suggestions have been tried and tested and found to work. Not every one is suited to every person and every situation, so please regard them as a menu that you can try out and from which you can choose the ones that work for you.

Part One

Strategic thinking

Chapter 1

Think strategically... to get a good degree!

What is 'strategic thinking'?

Here's what I mean by 'strategic thinking'.

Strategic thinking is thinking before acting. Strategic thinking is taking considered decisions rather than rushing in or behaving compulsively. Strategic thinking is looking ahead. Strategic thinking is taking an overview. Strategic thinking is thinking about how to make the best use of your time.

And strategic thinking makes the difference between getting an upper second-class degree and a lower second. Are you someone whose academic work is geared solely to your next 'deadline' for handing in a piece of work? Are you someone who, asked to write an essay comparing and contrasting A and B, hands in nothing more than two lists, one a list of the attributes of A and the other a list of the attributes of B? Are you someone who doesn't look at past exam papers until you're actually revising for this year's exams? Are you someone who, faced with an exam question on X, immediately starts writing down everything you know about X? Answer 'Yes' to all four of these questions and I can tell you – without knowing who you are or reading anything at all that you've written – that you are heading for a lower second or even a third-class degree.

In contrast, if you

- are aware of all the deadlines ahead of you, and have already checked out your next few tasks as well as the task that is currently preoccupying you
- respond to a 'compare and contrast' task by thinking about what criteria you should use, and why, and what the significance is of the differences between A and B, and then write about those
- get hold of past exam papers early in a course and cross-check between those and the content of the course as it progresses
- respond to an exam question on X by first of all thinking about what the examiners are looking for and then putting together a plan for your answer before you start writing

then I can tell you now that you stand a good chance of achieving an upper second or even a first-class degree.

Strategic thinkers are alert. They're always asking questions. 'What's going on here?' 'Why are we being asked to do this?' 'Why are we being told this?' They notice differences and changes, and ask how they came about and what their significance is. 'How is it that these two writers can come to such different conclusions?' They read between the lines, picking up not only the message but also the message behind the message.

Strategic thinkers are skilful 'time managers'. They are very aware of the 'shape' of their working week. They make full use of bits and pieces of time. They always have with them something to read or think about. They're very aware of deadline clashes: they make plans in advance for handling them, and then put these plans into effect.

You might sometimes be tempted to say 'To hell with it all!' and adopt the very simplest, most basic kind of strategy, that of working on nothing but what your next deadline demands. That would be a mistake. It is short-sighted in more ways than one. Where the deadline for one task is followed very shortly by that for another, you would be leaving yourself very little time for the second one, and where you have a mixture of short-duration and long-duration tasks, the latter will keep being pushed to the back of the queue.

If you don't make a habit of looking ahead to see what's coming, and plan for it, you're forever being taken by surprise. There are things you haven't done, and now haven't time for. Deadlines have crept up on you, with penalties if you don't get your work in on time. It's like constantly running after a bus that you never quite manage to catch. The consequence is a huge amount of stress. Your life could hardly be more stressful.

Strategic thinking cuts down stress. If you *do* look and plan ahead, you're much more in control. Certainly your life won't be free of stress – there are exams and other assessment hoops to jump through – but you have more choice, more autonomy, more freedom.

I meet many students who have been finding academic work frustrating and concluded that they just aren't up to it: when they learn to take a strategic approach they are much more in control, produce better work, and their frustration diminishes dramatically.

Chapter 2

The idea of a time-use strategy

A strategic approach to using time

Strategic thinking implies that you have a strategy for using your time – a 'time-use strategy', a plan for how you will use future time, time lying ahead of you. You can have an 'individual' time-use strategy, directed towards accomplishing a single task, to the point where you can say 'Done that!' and cross it off your to-do list. That point constitutes your objective. And you can have an 'overall' time-use strategy whereby at any given time you will have a number of individual strategies, coordinated, under way simultaneously.

You can think of a strategy as a way of mentally 'colonizing the future': mapping the future and staking out claims to portions of time. And, of course, by virtue of the fact that it specifies how you will use your time, a strategy also specifies how you will *not* use your time.

But a time-use strategy does more than simply 'earmark' a period of time for an objective-directed activity. That time has to be productive. So adopting a time-use strategy also involves doing the following things:

● Finding the time that you need in order to accomplish your task

● Committing yourself to making the effort necessary to accomplish your task

● Making sure that you comprehend exactly what it is that your task requires you to do (this is crucial)

● Getting hold of the physical resources – such as books, equipment and materials – that your task requires

● Finding an environment to work in that is conducive to accomplishing your task.

Time

In a time-use strategy, time is patently a central element. An individual strategy will specify the chronological sequence of steps that will take you to your objective and – at least in outline – allocate your time among those steps. An overall strategy will ration your time among the individual strategies that you are pursuing. Both individual and overall strategies may specify actual periods of time: a day or days in the calendar, times of day, and so on.

Commitment to making an effort

The quality of the effort you will be able to devote to your tasks will be measured chiefly by factors such as your ability to get started on a task, the undiluted attention you are able to give it, and your ability to resist distractions. Commitment is a psychological factor, a state of mind, and creating commitment involves motivating yourself and structuring incentives for yourself.

Comprehension of what your task requires you to do

It may seem obvious, but still needs stating: for your strategy to be effective you need to comprehend the nature of the task ahead of you. You need to comprehend two things:

1.   What is required of you, what your 'end product' is to be
2.   How to proceed, what steps to take, at least at the outset.

Often it will indeed be obvious what is required of you: you have to solve a problem, derive a proof, draw up a legal advice, and so on. But in the humanities and social sciences and other essay-based subjects, you are likely to be instructed to 'discuss', 'analyse', 'critically evaluate', 'comment' and the like, and here it is all too easy to take the nature of your task for granted, and to get it wrong. You may get your essay written and handed in on time – you attain your objective in that sense – but if you have not correctly comprehended what your teacher wants from you, your result – the mark you get – will disappoint you. So it is crucially important that your perceptions of the nature of your tasks are in line with what your teachers want. Accordingly you will find it helpful to have a supplementary strategy for eliciting from your teachers exactly what they want (or would be pleased to receive; they may not have a detailed vision of what they want) and for clearing up any uncertainty you may have.

Physical resources
Having the necessary physical resources – such as books, equipment and materials – to hand is a prerequisite for every task that you have to undertake. They will be particular to each task, and you should be given guidance by your teachers as to what you need. If such guidance is not forthcoming, you may have to do your own research in this respect. Indeed, even if you do get guidance there is no harm in looking around to see if there is anything else that you could usefully use.

Environment
Having a supportive physical and social environment can be crucial in enabling you to accomplish a task successfully. What kind of environment will be supportive will vary from person to person. Some prefer a room at home, others a library, others a café on the high street. If you have some choice in the matter, it would be sensible to experiment to find what suits you best.

Strategy: steps along a path

Essentially a strategy sets out a sequence of future activities – things to do – that you see as culminating in accomplishing your task. So you can think of your strategy as a path towards your objective. This path is made up of steps. The steps are of two kinds: events and stages.

Events are brief. Seen from a distance they are pretty much instantaneous, taking place at a moment in time. You take a decision – make a choice – about a topic for an essay; you print out your final version; you hand it in. Stages, in contrast, are where you spend time. If you're working on an essay, your stages might include doing the necessary reading, putting a rough draft together, assembling your final draft, editing and proofreading. All these are activities that take significant amounts of time.

Your strategy, then, will amount to a sequence of events and stages. Most will logically have to take place before the next one in the sequence can be started, so your sequence is in a chronological order, but it may be possible to carry out some stages 'in parallel': for example, where two independent steps have to be taken before a third can be.

Individual and overall strategies

We can think of an individual time-use strategy as a path towards a single objective. But it is very rare that you will find yourself with a single, solitary objective on your mind: usually only the most single-minded of PhD students will be in that position. At any given moment, you are likely to be following several paths. You can think of these paths as being amalgamated into a 'road', and your individual strategies as being amalgamated into an 'overall' strategy. An overall strategy accordingly serves as a kind of 'road map' into the future.

Designing an overall strategy is a quite complicated and difficult matter. It involves coordinating and putting together a number of individual strategies, each of which is competing for time with every other one. So designing an overall strategy involves first designing your individual strategies, and then making compromises to resolve the inevitable conflicting demands for your time, effort etc. Examples of how to do this are given later in this book, especially in Chapter 9 (Manage two or more tasks at once).

Commitment versus flexibility

A strategy starts out as an idea, a concept – something in your head. You probably flesh it out on paper or computer screen; you may talk to other people about it. Then, step by step, if all goes according to plan – if there's no slip 'twixt cup and lip – you implement your strategy.

It is most people's experience that, as they move along the path of a strategy, they become increasingly attached to whatever it is they are working on. They acquire commitment to it. If you choose an essay topic and then spend a week working on it, you feel increasingly committed to sticking with that topic and not switching to another – even if tempted – by virtue of the time and effort you have invested. Your commitment carries you through even if the going gets hard. You'll probably feel even more strongly committed if you've told other people which topic you've chosen, because to change would be to admit you'd made the wrong choice in the beginning, and that could be embarrassing.

Commitment, then, drives out flexibility. It reduces the range of options open to you. This creates a problem because following a strategy is also a learning process, and partly what you learn is that there exist pitfalls and problems that you hadn't anticipated. So you always have to balance your commitment against the need for flexibility, the need to keep some options open.

Chapter 3

Creating a time-use strategy

The context: working under pressure

As a student, you are always working under pressure. Pressures stem from the demands, expectations, duties and imperatives that are bearing down on you: from the institution, your teachers, your family. You have signed up to the higher education system, and if you want a degree you have to jump through the hoops that system sets for you; you have to accomplish the tasks that those hoops specify. Likewise family expectations and duties will set you certain tasks. Some will be identical with those of the institution – your family will usually want you to jump successfully through its hoops – but others will be competing with the institution's tasks: you may be expected to be caring for members of your family or to attend a family occasion out of the country during term time, for example.

You will also have your own personal aspirations and ambitions, stemming from your personal needs, drives and desires. These amount to a further set of pressures, internally generated ones. They might include getting a good degree, earning some money, spending time with friends, getting enough food and sleep, keeping reasonably fit and participating in a sport, and generally having a life. The academic aspiration among these – getting a good degree – implies that you will do more than just go through the motions of jumping through hoops: you will be aiming to achieve a certain standard.

From pressure to objective

Before you can create an overall time-use strategy, you need to have created your individual strategies. Before you can create individual strategies, you need to have identified your objectives. And, in order to be clear about those objectives, you need to be consciously aware of the pressures on you.

For many people, pressures are always at the back of their minds, never in the foreground, and they spend their lives reacting pretty much spontaneously – which means unthinkingly – to pressures, rather than responding to them in a strategic, thoughtful way. If this is how you behave, stop it at once! Move into 'strategy mode'.

You can begin right now. Take a pen and a sheet of paper. Draw a vertical line to divide the sheet of paper into two equal columns. At the top of the left-hand column write 'Pressures'; at the top of the right-hand one write 'Objectives'. In the left-hand column make a list of the pressures, of whatever kind and from whatever source, that you feel under right now. If you feel it, if it's on your mind as something you must do, it counts as a pressure, so put it on your list. The list will of course include academic pressures, the work you are expected to have done by the end of this week or next, all the family and social obligations you feel you should meet in the near future, and anything else that you feel at all pressurized by at the moment (for example, maybe you have to fill out applications for jobs or internships). On your list highlight – or put a cross by – those pressures that feel most onerous right now, most burdensome.

Now, alongside each item in that list, in the right-hand column, write down exactly what it is that the pressure is pressurizing you to *do*, and when.

This is your objective. (In a few cases the pressure may already be expressed very specifically, clearly and unambiguously, as an objective, in which case your entry in the right-hand column will be the same as that in the left-hand one.) What you are doing here is translating each pressure into a precise, specific objective.

Sometimes two pressures will give rise to one objective. For example, you might be under pressure from one of your teachers to hand in an essay on Friday week. That's a fairly basic objective. You might also feel strongly motivated to do really well in that subject. Adding that ambition could result in a modified objective: to hand in a grade A essay. It will be this more specific objective, as you have now expressed it and 'own' it, that will determine how much time you allocate to it in your time-use strategy.

Here are a couple more examples of the translation of pressures into specific objectives. You might feel a family duty to visit your grandparents within the coming month; this will translate into an objective to visit them on a specific day and perhaps spend a specific amount of time with them. You might aspire to getting into your college's basketball team; this could translate into an objective of improving your performance to the point where, if you are an attacker, you are consistently scoring more points than others in your team. (This makes the point that whether you actually attain an objective may depend on factors outside your control: the steps you take are on a path towards maximizing the likelihood – rather than actually ensuring – that you will attain that objective.)

From objective to time-use strategy

The procedure for getting from an objective to the individual time-use strategy that you need in order to attain that objective, is basically as follows

1. Check your task comprehension, resources and environment
2. 'Map out' your path to your objective
3. Make a realistic time estimate.

Let's look at the three elements of this procedure one by one.

1. Check your task comprehension, resources and environment

You must be sure that you comprehend what the task actually requires you to do: what your end product is to be, and what procedure – e.g. for solving a problem, getting started on an essay – you should be following. Even if you have a tried and tested procedure that has worked well many times before and should be applicable this time too, you need to assure yourself that it will be. If you don't already have that comprehension of your task, the first stage in your strategy will be to gain it. So ask your teachers, ask your fellow students, ask others who have taken that course in past years, ask anyone who might be able to help. Otherwise you'll probably be making assumptions, with the risk that they'll send you off on the wrong track, or just floundering about, in both cases resulting in a waste of your precious time.

Likewise it will be prudent to check whether you have the appropriate physical resources (books, equipment, materials) to hand, and will have a supportive physical and social environment in which to work. Take nothing for granted. If matters are not as you need them to be, it will be sensible to deal with the deficiency now – preferably by rectifying it – rather than run into trouble later on. That 'trouble' could take the form of a major disruption to your time-use strategy.

2. 'Map out' your path to your objective

Once you have identified your objective, and checked for task comprehension, resources and environment, you have to identify and make a 'map' of the path that will take you to it. That is, you have to work out what steps – events and stages – are necessary to get you to that objective from where you are now. You need to identify, one by one, the sequence of moment-in-time events and time-consuming stages along that path.

Let's take an example. If you have an essay to write, your steps might be as follows:

1. Identify a range of possible topics
2. Choose (decide on) a topic
3. Analyse your chosen topic
4. Review the literature
5. Put a rough draft together
6. Print out your rough draft

7. Sleep on it

8. Upgrade, polish and proofread your draft

9. Check that all your references are properly cited

10. Print out the essay

11. Hand it in.

(This list is not a model for you to follow. It contains some imperfections, as noted below.)

Likewise, before you get to visit your grandparents you'll probably have to (1) clear a space in your diary; (2) check that that day will be a convenient one for them and fix on a good time for you to arrive; (3) arrange transport or check the bus/train timetable; and (4) on the day actually leave in time to get there at the appointed hour. And before you can get into your college's basketball team you will have to (1) attend practice sessions regularly; (2) work your way up through junior teams; and (3) make yourself available for matches.

Now go back to the list of objectives that you made just now. Choose one, and 'map' the sequence of steps – the events and stages – that you will have to go through to attain that objective. These events and stages have got to be specific, precise – not vague and general. That should not pose any problem with events. If you have to hand in an essay by 5 pm on 16 March 2007, or catch the 16.05 from London Paddington to Penzance on 12 September 2007, the requisite event is absolutely clear-cut: you know exactly what you have to do, and if you miss the essay deadline or the train you know without a shadow of doubt that you've missed it.

Stages require more thought. Let's say you have an essay to write, on a topic that you have chosen, and that you have been given a reading list. You might have written down as your stage 4, as in the model above, 'Review the literature'. That is simply not good enough. As an element in a time-use strategy it is completely useless, because it is so unspecific and open-ended. It's not telling you what you are going to *do* with the literature – are you intending to absorb every word? – and it's giving you no indication whatever of how much time you need to allocate to this stage or how you will know when you've done enough and can move on. Reviewing the literature thoroughly with a view to mastering it could take you several weeks, or even months, if there's a lot of it, and if you let it.

So think about what you're going to do with the literature. If there are specialist terms (language) in the topic, you could (4a) look in the recommended books for definitions of these terms. You could (4b) scan introductory chapters for useful 'overview' statements on the lines of 'The explanations that have been put forward for Muslim separatism in pre-1947 India fall into four distinct categories ...'. If the topic touches on a current academic debate, you could (4c) take the most recent articles and look specifically for references to that debate. And/or you could (4d) check out the conclusions that the different authors come to for similarities and differences. Doing any of these will require only a limited time: you will know clearly what you have to do, and when you have done it you will know you have done it. And while you will probably have to make further use of the literature, after completing those component stages you will know what you are looking for and be able to make a realistic estimate of the time you'll need.

3. Make a realistic time estimate

Start by making an estimate, as realistic as you can manage and drawing on your previous experience of working on similar tasks, of the time you think you'll require for each stage along your path. You could make this calculation in terms of days or hours. If you have a deadline two weeks or more away, you'll probably find it convenient to divide up the intervening time by days, effectively setting yourself intermediate deadlines over the two weeks. If your deadline is closer, you'll want to work in terms of hours.

Now add your 'stage times' together to give yourself a 'total time'. Then take a close look at how your total time is allocated among the various stages in your strategy. Bear in mind that your deadline will feel less oppressive early on, and that if you 'overrun' in the early stages, that's time lost to the later ones. In extremis, you can always grab time from later stages if you really need it, but you'll have no such luxury later on if you've been frittering time away. Bear in mind too that academic work tends to expand to fill whatever time is available. So reassess your time allocation among stages. You might like to be more 'tight-fisted' with your time where the early stages are concerned.

Being realistic also requires you to face up to uncertainty. You will almost certainly be less clear about what work will be entailed in some stages as opposed to others. With reading and any other kind of investigative work you never know what you are going to find, so you might like to add a 'contingency allowance' stage to give you time to deal with the unexpected. Then you can take time from your contingency allowance if you need it. This is of course a more systematic and organized way of responding to the unexpected than grabbing time from later stages.

Time-requirement and progress charts

Your time requirement for an individual time-use strategy can be represented visually, very straightforwardly, in the form of a chart. An example is shown in Figure 3.1, taking as a case study the series of steps listed above that you might follow in producing an essay, any essay, where you have been able to choose the topic. (For simplicity, stage 4 has not been broken down into component parts, and I have not included a 'contingency allowance' stage.)

The precise lengths of the seven time-consuming stages in this particular example have no significance. The differences in length reflect nothing more than the general expectation that reviewing the literature and upgrading, polishing and proofreading your draft will take more time than any of the other stages, and that identifying a range of possible topics, analysing the chosen topic and sleeping on the rough draft will take less time. When you are formulating your strategy for producing a particular

Figure 3.1 Chart representing an individual time-use strategy

Key: The numbers denote steps. Events are shown as heavy bars and identified by numbers in brackets; stages as cells. Every cell in the chart represents a stage except the cell between steps (10) and (11).

Steps: (1) Identify a range of possible topics; (2) Choose (decide on) a topic; (3) Analyse your chosen topic; (4) Review the literature; (5) Put a rough draft together; (6) Print out your rough draft; (7) Sleep on it; (8) Upgrade, polish and proofread your draft; (9) Check that all your references are properly cited; (10) Print out the essay; (11) Hand it in.

essay, however, you can assign a target period of so many hours to each stage, or a target date by which you aim to complete it. You can then use the chart as a 'progress chart', marking off each stage as you complete it, and referring to it every so often to see whether you are keeping up with your schedule – or even ahead of it!

Reiteration yes; repetition no

I have presented the idea of a time-use strategy as a linear progression, where you move on smoothly from one stage to the next. Real life rarely runs so smoothly. We all find ourselves back-tracking at some point: going back to consult sources to see if we had properly understood something we had read; checking on early results; retracing our steps and going along a different route, and so on. Reiteration like this is perfectly normal, and if you find yourself doing it don't give yourself a hard time, don't feel there is something wrong with your methods.

What *is* to be avoided, however, is repetition. Repeating something in the hope that you'll get a different answer, and especially repeating it over and over again, wastes time; it is not constructive.

So when you're pursuing a time-use strategy, every now and again stand back and observe your pattern of work. If you find yourself repeating what you have already done and getting to a place where you have already been, you need to stop and find a way out of the repetitive 'loop'.

Divergence and convergence

When you're thinking about progressing a task through the various steps in your strategy, there are other progressions over time that you should be aware of. Especially in the early stages, you will be extending the 'scope' of what you are doing. You will be expanding your store of knowledge, theories and ideas; enlarging your grasp of the literature; exploring adjoining issues; collecting more data; doing more calculations; carrying out more trials and tests. You are operating in what might be called 'divergence' mode.

As you progress, however, you need to move in the opposite direction, to narrow the scope of what you are doing. You need to 'zero in' on what will be your finished product. As you become clearer what that product will be, you filter out material that you won't be using. You have a clearer idea of what knowledge, theories and ideas are relevant, and are able to exclude from your thoughts those that aren't. You are now operating in 'convergence' mode.

When you are planning a time-use strategy for a task, and allocating time for the various stages, it will pay you to bear divergence and convergence in mind. Allow for divergence in the early stages: it can be bewildering and disorientating as your task seems to expand, perhaps exponentially, in scope. Don't put convergence off too long. It can't be accomplished in an instant, it takes time; and if you leave it until the last minute you will be unable to meet your deadline.

Overall time-use strategies and management

Up to now I have been talking about individual time-use strategies – that is to say, strategies for accomplishing a single task, attaining a single objective. In real life, of course, as you'll be very well aware, students who are taking an undergraduate or taught master's degree are hardly ever in a position to be able to concentrate single-mindedly on a single task. Tackling a number of tasks simultaneously would seem to require an 'overall' time-use strategy, and this is something that is covered in Part Two of this book, especially Chapter 9 (Manage two or more tasks at once). In practice, it raises a number of issues that usually have to be resolved at the level of implementation, using day-to-day management techniques. I deal with these in the next chapter, Chapter 4.

Chapter 4

Implementing a time-use strategy

Issues, decisions, strategies and techniques

When it comes to the practicalities of making best use of your time, you find that you are faced with issues, 'What should I do?' questions. Your time-use strategies will have taken you some way to resolving these issues – answering these questions – but these strategies still remain to be implemented.

Once you've created a time-use strategy, it exists in your head or on paper or in electronic form but it has yet to be put into effect. While you are creating your strategy, you are planning ahead, planning what you will do at future points in time. It is when you actually arrive at those points that you are in the business of putting your strategy into effect, implementing it. As we saw in Chapter 3, when you are creating a time-use strategy you have certain decisions to take. It is the same when you are implementing your strategy: you have more decisions to take. These are day-to-day, on-the-spot decisions. You make them by applying an appropriate technique, which usually involves getting hold of information and then processing it in some way, and then taking a decision about what to do. You then act on the decision, either immediately or soon after.

For example, you might ask yourself: 'What shall I do first today?' You might then draw up a list of alternatives – A, B and C, the different tasks competing for your attention – and work out the likely outcome of starting with A or B or C. You would then make your decision, choosing one of those alternatives on the basis of which outcome you like best. (Or perhaps you have already placed A, B and C in order of priority, so you make your decision by choosing the alternative that is at the top of your priority list.) And then you would act on your decision.

In the following chapters I deal with a range of 'How to ...' issues. Each chapter offers a range of techniques for both creating strategy and implementing it.

Part Two

How to...

Chapter 5

Work out how much time you've got... and find more

How many hours in your week?

First of all, without doing any calculations have a guess at how many hours of 'your own time' you have available for academic work in a typical week. (By 'your own time' I mean time not taken up with formal teaching or time when your presence is not required in the classroom or laboratory or workshop, or out on fieldwork.) Have a quick guess at how much of 'your own time' you had in a typical week mid-term.

Now think back to your last full term-time week, Sunday to Saturday or Monday to Sunday. (If you're actually on vacation right now, cast your mind back to a typical mid-term week during the last term or semester.) How much of your own time did you have during that week? Do the sums. In total, there were 168 hours in that week. Subtract academic hours that weren't your own, i.e. that you spent in lectures or seminars and so on, where your attendance was required. Then subtract the time taken up by sleeping, eating, personal care and house-keeping; by travel to and from uni (unless you were able to use travel time for studying); by leisure activities; by paid work if you do paid work; and by any inescapable obligations involving your family, friends or faith. From the remainder, subtract any remaining oddments of time of half an hour or less.

Now subtract any periods of time when, despite being awake and not otherwise occupied, you were not in any condition to do academic work: you were fatigued from doing paid work or playing sport, or recovering from other leisure activities, perhaps. And then subtract those other periods when you had meant to do some academic work but didn't.

How much time have you got left now? And how close is that figure to your earlier guess? If you're within five hours, you're doing pretty well in the realism department. If your guessed-at figure is ten or more hours above your calculated figure – and especially if you're surprised by that – then you could do with being much more aware of where your time is going.

Finding more time for yourself

Now that you can see where your time is going, you can judge whether you need to find some more time for yourself. This means clawing it back from the activities and people demanding it.

Leisure activities
Think about which of your leisure activities you are finding most rewarding and which least. Can you drop the least rewarding, or reduce your involve-ment in them? Ask yourself which activities would be easiest to drop out of – for a time, at least; the answer to that question could depend on whether there are other people who could step into your place. You may find that activities in student societies are easiest to manage in this way because your fellow students are more understanding of the situation you're in.

Paid work
You'll probably find the demands of paid work more and more oppressive as exams approach. If you're thinking about this at the beginning of the aca-demic year, it's a good idea to work out how much you need to earn in the

year and then try to earn it in the first four or five months if possible. It's also sensible to look for work that you can switch off from at the end of your shift: you don't want to be thinking about it when you're not being paid to do so. Time of day is also important: if you are going to be physically tired when you finish work it's preferable for your hours of work to be late in the day so you can get some sleep at the end of your shift rather than have to turn to study.

Family and friendship obligations

Families are notorious for making demands, especially on women, that take no account of your need for study time. In addition, family members are often very poor at respecting your study space. Make it clear that your course does require you to study in your own time, and that it's necessarily a solitary activity that requires your concentration and undivided attention. I suggest that you start by seeing if you can negotiate an agreement that you be left undisturbed for certain times in the day and/or week.

If negotiation doesn't work out satisfactorily – if you can't reach an agreement, or if you do reach one but it isn't respected – try setting boundaries, unilaterally: 'This is when I'm available; this is when I am not.' You may need to 'patrol' these boundaries with some determination, to resist attempts to test and infringe them. Outside the boundaries, do your best to be really nice and helpful and cooperative, of course!

If setting boundaries doesn't work, your last resort – if it is available to you – is to absent yourself. Find somewhere away from the family home where you can work. Even then, keep regular hours so your family can accustom themselves to your pattern of life and work. You may find that after a while matters improve to the point where you can re-enter the family domain and have your boundaries respected.

Friends may make heavy demands too, especially if you are a 'good listener' or someone who is seen as 'motherly', a person on whose shoulder they can cry and to whom they can pour out their woes. It may be difficult to resist them, especially if their dependence on you makes you feel valued. But you must realize that they are placing a heavy burden on you, and it takes its toll on your 'emotional energy' as well as taking your time and distracting you from your own work and other concerns. As with your family, you need to try to negotiate times when you will and won't be available and, if this doesn't work, set boundaries. People who don't respect these are definitely not genuine friends of yours. They are 'dumping' their misery on you, and taking advantage of your good nature. You will find it difficult to tell them to get lost, but if you don't – albeit in more tactful language – you will be taking care of them at the expense of taking care of yourself.

Using travel time and 'fragments'

In the last working week, how much time did you spend travelling each working day? Were you able to use any of this time for working?

If your daily journey involves being seated in a bus or train for more than 20 minutes, that could add up to more than 3 hours a week of potential work time. You may want these fragments of time for relaxing, or for planning or going over your day; some people like to use the journey as a 'buffer' between home and uni. Others, however, like to use it as a 'bridge' – especially the homeward journey, so as not to switch off from 'study mode'. Be aware of the possibility of using your journey for preparing for a lecture or seminar, or going over notes that you've taken, or just for reading. It's a good idea to always carry something to read. Bus or train hold-ups are much easier to bear if you can read while you wait.

How fragmented is your working week? In a typical term-time week, how many stretches of (a) 30 minutes to 1 hour, and (b) 1–2 hours of your 'own' time did you have? Do you think you made good use of these fragments?

It will help you if you can be aware of how fragmented your 'own' time is, and of how good you have been up to now at making use of the smaller fragments. If you have not been good at this – perhaps you like to have two or more hours at your disposal so you can have a good 'run' at a task – then there are two lessons for you. First, you should guard those precious longer stretches and try to avoid them being nibbled away at by small tasks. Second, train yourself to make use of those smaller fragments. Always have with you something to read or work on or think about: a book or article, a past exam paper, a problem, an outline for an essay you're about to start work on. And you must have a pen and paper or a laptop or electronic notebook with you at such times too, of course. With practice, you'll find it easier to 'switch on and off' – to pick a task up again where you left off – and thus to use those smaller fragments to the full.

'The road to hell is paved with good intentions'

Do you sometimes – frequently? – set aside time for working (e.g. after your evening meal) but then *not* use it for working – perhaps because you didn't feel up to it or because an opportunity to do something else presented itself?

The purpose of asking you this question is not to draw attention to any supposed moral deficiencies on your part – don't beat yourself up if you're not happy with your answer – but to get you to take a close look at your ability to make realistic judgements as to what your levels of energy and strength of motivation will be a few hours ahead.

It is important that you know your limitations, and – if you aren't in a position to rectify them – tailor your work plans to them. If evenings after dinner or supper are not good times for you to work, you have to find time elsewhere. Maybe have a sandwich when you have your afternoon break and postpone your evening meal by an hour? Be creative!

If the temptation to do other things besides work is irresistible, then you could also look for means of keeping out of temptation's way.

How long until ...?

In addition to working out how much time you have available for studying in a typical week, you will frequently find yourself calculating how long you have until a deadline for submitting work or taking an exam. Such a deadline may seem a long way away ... until you do the sums and realize how much of the intervening time you are going to need for other things. So add up the number of days until the deadline, then subtract those days or parts of days that won't be available for studying. Now fit a 'time-requirement chart' for your task (see page 23) into the remaining days and you will see that the number of days available for each stage is only a fraction of the total number of days to the deadline. (For more on this, see the next chapter.) If you're revising for, say, four exams, divide the number of available days by four to give you available days per exam ... and give yourself a fright! That should get your adrenalin going.

Chapter 6

Plan your weekly routine

Why you need a routine

Most people find it a great help to have a regular routine during the academic term/semester. Students who are effective workers seem to make it a central element of their time-use strategy. Indeed, the routine for any given week provides a 'frame' in which your strategies for individual tasks will fit together. A routine will provide a rhythm and stability to your life, which you'll probably find reassuring. People without routines are liable to find themselves staying up all night to finish a piece of work by the deadline, then sleeping late and missing lectures and classes, and consequently getting further and further behind, until they are facing a crisis. Although you may still be taken by surprise and knocked sideways when unscheduled events happen, if you are in control of most elements of your life you may find it easier to deal with those unscheduled events. Having a routine also enables you to see what scope you have for fitting in non-routine work that has to be handed in by a deadline.

To some extent a routine is forced on you by timetabled events where your attendance is required – these usually follow the same pattern each week – but you may find it advantageous to create a routine for yourself 'out of hours', when you aren't actually compelled to. This is especially so because most academic tasks require thinking, and thinking takes time – and unpredictable amounts of time at that. And the academic life isn't one where you can take each day as it comes, where you can wake up each morning, wonder what you'll do today, and just get on and do it: that would be the intellectual equivalent of going on a white-water rafting trip, and equally likely to generate both spills and thrills.

Getting into a regular pattern of work is easiest if you become familiar with it in all its aspects. So don't just do it; *see* yourself doing it, make a picture. And the simplest kind of picture to make is of course a chart of your timetable.

Your official timetable

The first thing you need when organizing and making a picture of your weekly routine is your official timetable. This will probably be notified to you in the form of a list. As soon as you get it, transform it into a chart. Start with a blank diagram as shown in Figure 4.1, covering every hour in every day in your normal working week. Typically this might cover 9 am to 6 pm Monday to Friday.

Now mark on the chart your fixed (timetabled) slots, those where your attendance is required – or at least expected. Do this by marking them on your chart, preferably using different colours of ink or highlighter to distinguish your different subjects and (if you have enough colours) your lectures, classes, seminars, tutorials, lab sessions, or whatever. You now have a chart of your official timetable.

Just a glance at this official timetable will show you (a) where your days are crowded with teaching sessions; (b) where you have one teaching session followed by another with no gap between; (c) where you have a 'long' day, with (say) a 9 am start and a 6 pm finish; and (d) where you have significant

	Monday	Tuesday	Wednesday	Thursday	Friday
9–10					
10–11					
11–12					
12–1					
1–2					
2–3					
3–4					
4–5					
5–6					

Figure 4.1 Blank timetable for the working week

chunks of your 'own' time. You ought to become very familiar with this pattern; doing that should take no effort on your part.

Your 'super-timetable'

Although your officially timetabled slots will be confined to something like normal working hours in the normal working week – Monday to Friday, 9 am to 6 pm, for example – almost every student does academic work outside these hours, and in many places libraries and computer rooms are open until 11 pm or even later the whole week round; indeed, 24-hour opening is not unknown.

So construct a 'super-timetable' grid for all of your waking hours. If you're never up in the morning before 8 am and never up later than 2 am, your blank grid will look like the one in Figure 4.2.

To use your super-timetable, first mark on it those times when you are absolutely not going to do academic work. These could be set mealtimes in your hall of residence, times that you set aside for religious practices,

	Mon.	Tues.	Wed.	Thurs.	Fri.	Sat.	Sun.
8–9							
9–10							
10–11							
11–12							
12–1							
1–2							
2–3							
3–4							
4–5							
5–6							
6–7							
7–8							
8–9							
9–10							
10–11							
11–12							
12–1							
1–2							

Figure 4.2 Blank 'super-timetable' for all waking hours

Saturday nights out and times when you have to do paid work. With the latter, be realistic if you need extra time for 'recovery' – does paid work leave you tired or raring to get back to your books?

Next, mark on your super-timetable everything that's on your official timetable.

Now there's something else you can very usefully do. Identify necessary – or at least desirable – activities that are 'ancillary' to your timetabled formal teaching sessions: (a) things it would be good to do *before* those sessions, like preparing; (b) things it would be good to do *after* those sessions, like writing up, to follow up and consolidate what you have gained from the session; and (c) things you need to do *between* sessions, like tackling problem exercises after a lecture and before the subsequent class.

Before

For each of your sessions, ask yourself – and write down your answers – what you need to do beforehand. What do you need to prepare for, and what do you need to do by way of preparation? You will almost always be expected to prepare for a class or seminar or tutorial. In quantitative subjects and others taught in a 'problem-centred' way, there will be problems to tackle or exercises to do before a class. For classes in other subjects, again you will be expected to have done some work so you can make a contribution. For lectures, too, consider whether you would benefit from doing some reading or looking up beforehand, to make it easier for you to take on board what the lecturer is saying. For example, if you brief yourself in advance about any specialized terminology the lecturer is likely to use, during the lecture itself you won't get distracted by asking yourself: 'What does X mean?'

When are you going to do this preparation work? First estimate how much time in consecutive hours (e.g. a one-, two- or three-hour period) you will need before each class/seminar or lecture. Now inspect your super-timetable to see where you can fit these periods in. You might want to aim to keep them as single blocks of time if you can; otherwise think about how to split them up without fragmenting them too much. In some cases you will probably find time the day or evening before; in others you may find time earlier the same day. Many people find the best time is immediately before the session, but this will not be possible first thing in the morning or when one session is immediately followed by another.

There may of course be some kinds of preparation, like problems set as homework, where you can't be sure how long they will take you, so you may want to set time aside for them well before the relevant class. Then if you don't complete them within that time period, you'll have the possibility of grabbing some time later. Indeed, you could build in a contingency allowance somewhere in your super-timetable so you have 'spare' time available if you need it.

After

What do you need to do *after* each formal teaching session? You might want to go over notes that you have made to check whether they are complete and whether you have 'captured' and understood everything. It's a way of 'consolidating' what you've learned. You can do it either by yourself or with other people who have attended the session. If you do it with other people you stand a better chance of resolving problems, and you'll probably enjoy working in a collaborative way – there are few opportunities for anything approaching teamwork in UK higher education. It would probably be best to do this as soon after the session as possible, while it is fresh in your mind. Again, you will have to decide how much time to allow for it.

Between

If you have work like problem exercises that you need to do on your own between (say) a lecture and a class, you are free to choose a time for them that is convenient for you. The only constraint is that if you aren't sure how long they will take you, you may not want to leave it until the last moment to tackle them. On the other hand, of course, leaving them until fairly late is a way of rationing the amount of time you will spend on them – an example of 'deadline rationing'.

▼ ▼ ▼

Now allocate times for all these ancillary activities and mark them on your super-timetable. This requires thought, because there will be clashes to resolve, as when formal teaching sessions run consecutively, with no gaps between them. You will have to decide what to do when. There will also be other considerations to take into account, especially to do with work that does not fit neatly into your weekly framework.

If you can do so without creating problems for yourself, try to leave yourself some decent-sized chunks of time that you can use for working on more substantial tasks, such as (a) assignments that will be assessed, whether as part of a continuous assessment regime or in an ad hoc, one-off way; and (b) tasks that you want to carry out and hand in for the purpose of getting feedback from your teachers. Both of these require care and more than odd scraps of time if you are to do yourself justice and earn your teachers' respect.

Your working week

You're not quite finished yet with planning your weekly routine. When you've got this far, stand back and look at the pattern of your super-time-table. Do you have one or more 'free' days? And other days that are quite busy?

If your Monday is free and your Tuesday and Wednesday are busy, you might want to use the Monday to prepare for the next two days, and save your weekend for work on one-off assignments. Or, if your Friday afternoon is free, you could use that time for preparation and preserve your precious whole day on Monday.

If you have the whole of Friday free, you might like to bring your weekend forward to Friday/Saturday and use Sunday to prepare for the week ahead.

It's at this point, while you're organizing your working week, that you might like to think about what are your best times of day for working. Some people find they work best in the mornings, and like to make an early start. Others find night-time is best, especially after everyone else has gone to bed and everything is quiet. Whichever you find best, save those times for work, and use other times of day for things like shopping, housework, personal care and going to the gym. Mark your work and non-work times on your super-timetable too.

Whatever you do, use your imagination, spot opportunities and make the most of them. You will find it enormously helpful to your career as a student to have a comfortable pattern to your working week, a regular rhythm that suits you. An extra benefit of having a routine is that it makes it easier to defend your working time against encroachments. And if other people know what your routine is, they will find it easier to respect your need for time for yourself. See the following chapters for suggestions for sticking to your routine and stopping other activities from infringing on the times you've allocated.

Creating a routine for the vacation

At the end of term or semester, many students have plans for doing academic work during the vacation, especially for catching up on their studies. Sadly, these plans are often not fully realized. In the Christmas and Easter vacations, family get-togethers claim time and attention, work gets put off and then the end of the vacation is just round the corner.

There is a less recognized disrupting factor that sets in straight after the end of term. In the last week of term there are always deadlines to meet, work to hand in, end-of-term parties, plans for the vacation to be made, and a general air of excitement. Immediately afterwards – usually in the first few weekdays of the vacation – there is invariably a sense of anti-climax. Energy levels fall; everyone suffers from 'adrenalin slump'.

This state of mind and body is not conducive to revving up for a programme of work. If you try to get down to work straight away you will almost certainly find it a chore and a drag, your heart won't be in it, and you won't be working efficiently. So when you're planning to study during the vacation, I suggest you allow yourself three or four days at the beginning to regain your energy, before getting down to work. Then establish a routine for yourself, and make it known to those around you.

In terms of a work strategy, you may want to do a little work on some subjects first to get them out of the way, so you can concentrate on others. Or you might want to start with those that are giving you most difficulty. There is no set rule to follow, except to be aware of what you are doing and in control; don't let any one subject 'suck' your energy and time away and leave you with nothing for the others.

For ideas on planning a work strategy if you have catching up to do, see Chapter 16. In the Christmas vacation, if you haven't got catching up to do, and you're up to date with your assignments, think about doing some preparation for next term's work, especially in any courses that you're finding hard.

But do take some time off during your vacations. You don't want to return to university in a burned-out state. If you don't manage to get a change of scenery, at least try to take it easy for a few days before coming back.

Monitor and review

As with every other suggestion in this book, see how well your super-timetable works for you. Almost certainly, your first try will need to be amended as you realize where you have allowed more or less time than you need.

Chapter 7

Watch those deadlines

Deadlines

Do your deadlines frighten you? They are a fact of every student's life, so it is important to face up to them. Mark them up on a wallchart, so you see them every day, and the likelihood is that they will lose their capacity to frighten you – a much better solution than hiding them out of sight.

Your weekly super-timetable (see Chapter 6) should enable you to keep up to date with your learning and any weekly continuous regime to which you are subjected. But on top of your regular routine there will be superimposed 'one-off' tasks that require you to submit assignments, take tests and give presentations on or by set dates, 'deadlines'. It is crucially important for you to be very aware of your deadlines. You can't afford to have a deadline sneak up on you or have it take you by surprise.

You need to be particularly alert for deadlines that coincide, because that situation is very demanding on your time and attention (see Chapter 9 on managing two or more tasks at once). If you have any say in the matter, try to avoid that happening. Always be aware of what deadlines you have coming up in the next few weeks. Then if one of your teachers asks you to do a presentation in three weeks' time, and you know you already have an assignment to hand in on that date, you can immediately ask to do your presentation on a different date. If you don't respond immediately, you may lose the chance of a different date.

The invaluable wallchart

Keep a note of your deadlines in two places: in your diary or electronic personal assistant (if you have one), to carry around with you, and on a wallchart (or year planner) stuck in a conspicuous position on the wall of your room – somewhere where you can't help but see it. When you're informed of a new deadline, immediately write it in your diary and – especially – mark it on your wallchart. Your deadlines need to be ever present in your consciousness, so use colours and bold markings to make your wallchart visually striking.

There's something else to mark in your diary and on your wallchart: the numbers of the weeks of term or semester. A convenient way of doing this is to number the Mondays. Put a 1 on the first Monday of term, a 2 on the second Monday, and so on. You may find it a good idea to 'register' all your deadlines in that way. So you can remind yourself: 'I've got a presentation to do in Week 8 and an assessed essay to hand in during Week 9.'

Chapter 8

Estimate how long a task will take

How good are you at making time estimates?

If you are someone who, before starting a task with a deadline attached, consciously makes an estimate of how long it will take you, you are a very unusual person indeed. Most of us, including students, will do one of the following:

- If it's a task that genuinely interests us, get stuck into it straight away.

- Take a quick look at it, to check whether there's anything out of the ordinary about it, and then stick it in a queue of 'things to be done'.

- Get round to it *either* when it reaches the top of the 'things to be done' queue *or* when you feel it has become urgent, whichever is the sooner. (The feeling of urgency probably comes on when you sense that the time it will probably take is close to the time you have available.)

Whichever of these methods you employ, the test is whether you hand in the piece of work by the deadline *and* you are satisfied by the quality of it. (Handing in rubbish, even if you meet the deadline, doesn't count!)

So, think back to a half-dozen or so of your most recent experiences in trying to meet deadlines, and let me ask you:

- How many of those deadlines did you meet?
- Of those deadlines that you did meet, was it a struggle to meet them?
- When you met a deadline, did you feel the quality of your work would have been better if you'd had more time?
- Did you ever find yourself giving a presentation that you felt insufficiently prepared for?
- Of those experiences, in how many were you taken by surprise by how long it took you to complete a task and hand it in?

I must emphasize that the purpose of these questions is not to expose any human frailty or inadequacy on your part. It is to help you face up to whatever is the reality for you, a necessary prerequisite to making improvements in your use of time. So if you have a tendency to miss deadlines or to struggle to meet them, if you feel the pressure of time limits the quality of your work, and especially if being taken by surprise is a recurring feature of your student experience, the first thing to do is to recognize and acknowledge these facts and feelings. Then you can start to move forward.

What I suggest is that you do make a conscious effort to estimate how long a task will take you. But first you may like to consider the possibility of doing without a time estimate.

Doing without a time estimate

Let's say, for the sake of example, that you have an essay to write and your hand-in date is two weeks away. You could, if you felt like it, just make a start in a fairly relaxed way – after all, two weeks is a long time in academia, is it not? – and rely on the approach of your deadline to give you an increased sense of urgency later.

This is indeed a time-use strategy, of a sort. But it leaves you very vulnerable to the unexpected and tempts you to spend a disproportionate amount of time on the early stages, especially reviewing the literature and putting a rough draft together. Not only will you spend a disproportionate amount of time on these tasks – you will have no incentive to think carefully about how you use that time. Even if you don't run into unforeseen difficulties, you are likely to be pushed for time when you come to upgrade, polish and proofread your draft and check your references, so the piece of work you hand in is not likely to do justice to your ability.

Formulating a strategy

So let's assume that you are prepared to try to make a conscious effort to estimate how long a task will take you. But don't just pluck a figure – a number of hours or days – out of the air: you have to do some thinking and calculating. Indeed, you need to formulate – in outline, at least – a *strategy*.

Begin with task comprehension. Before you can estimate how long a task will take you, you need to have a good idea of what kind of task it is: what is expected of you and how you are going to proceed. If you don't possess this knowledge, you will have to allow some time for researching it – and indeed you may not be able to go further until you have done so. You also need to check that the physical resources that you need are available. If they aren't, it will take time to get hold of them.

Next, make a list of the steps – the events and the time-taking stages – that you'll need to take to accomplish your task. Now take each stage, one by one, and examine it carefully. First, see if you can break each one down into component parts, smaller stages. I gave the example earlier of breaking down 'Reviewing the literature' into four component stages: (a) looking in the recommended books for definitions of specialist terms; (b) scanning introductory chapters for useful 'overview' statements; (c) looking for references to a current academic debate; and/or (d) checking out the conclusions that the different authors come to for similarities and differences.

Now inspect each of your stages and, if you can easily do so, allocate the requisite period of time (days or hours) to it. If you can do this for all your stages, then estimating how long your task will take is simply a matter of adding together the time you expect to require for each stage.

If you can't easily allocate a period of time to all your stages, that is likely to be because the difficult ones are 'open-ended'. For example, you might have a stage of 'background reading' or 'collecting data' that could drag on for several weeks if you had nothing else to do. If you do let it drag on, you're in trouble. You're in 'divergence mode': your material and your thoughts and possibly your collection of notes are growing and growing, and you're leaving yourself with less and less time to 'converge' on completing your task. So, difficult though it may be, it is really important that you find a way of allocating time to open-ended stages.

Allocating time to an open-ended stage

There are basically two strategies you can use to allocate a period of time to an open-ended stage: you can set yourself a deadline, or you can say to yourself, 'I need a minimum of so many hours/days for this.'

Setting yourself a deadline
This is the strategy to use if you feel there is no point in making an estimate of how long the stage will take – it will take as long as you let it. What you have to do in that situation is to set a limit to it – a deadline – and this will have to be quite arbitrary. So you might say: 'I will give myself until Wednesday night for this, then – irrespective of where I've got to – I'll move on to the next stage. But I'll leave myself some "contingency time" later in my schedule so that I can come back to it and do some more work if necessary. If I do return to it later, I would expect to have a clearer idea of what I need to do.'

Specifying an absolute minimum
The second, alternative strategy for dealing with an open-ended stage is to ask yourself: 'What is the absolute minimum I have to do before I can move on to the next stage?' There might be just one book and two articles that you need to scan to find relevant extracts, or just a pilot sample of data that will be sufficient for the moment. Again, you would need to leave yourself

contingency time later so that you can return to that stage and do more work: find more extracts from the literature or extend your sample of data.

▼ ▼ ▼

As you can see, whichever of these strategies you adopt, reiteration plays an important part. Always build an allowance of contingency time into your strategy and don't ever be afraid of using it for 'reiterative loops'. If you think back to your experiences of learning, I am sure you'll recollect times when you've gone back to something and found that on a second reading or practice you had a better understanding of it, or you had acquired a skill that eluded you the first time round.

Once you have allocated time to your open-ended stages and your contingency allowance you can add up the total time you require for your task to give you your estimate of how long it will take you.

Rationing your time between stages

You aren't quite finished yet, however. It's sensible to check your strategy by looking at the distribution of your time among the stages. In particular, pay attention to the balance between 'divergence' and 'convergence' (see Chapter 3). If you are working with a great deal of new material, you must take care not to let the divergence stages go on so long that you have left yourself insufficient time for convergence on to your finished product. You may want to split your stages into ones of alternate divergence and convergence to avoid this happening.

Monitoring and review

You will find it useful – in the world of work as well as the academic world – to monitor and review your competence at estimating the time you will need for tasks. So when you start a task keep a record of your time estimate, and when you complete it see how accurate your estimate has been. If you have overshot your estimate, see if you can see why this happened, and try to make a better estimate next time.

▼ ▼ ▼

PS: Is there something holding you back from handing in work by the deadline? If so, see Chapter 14: Stop being such a perfectionist.

Chapter 9

Manage two or more tasks at once

The 'interleaving' strategy

In considering the demand for a time-use strategy, we have so far discussed individual tasks and thus individual strategies. In real life, of course, as you'll be very well aware, students who are taking an undergraduate or taught master's degree are hardly ever in a position to be able to concentrate single-mindedly on a single task. So now let's move on to the problem of how to cope with two or more tasks at once. This will require you to have an overall time-use strategy.

You have a kind of jigsaw puzzle to solve, with the added twist that you will have to design many of the pieces yourself. What you inevitably find is that your individual strategies are competing with one another for time, so you have to ration your time among them. Thus your overall strategy is constrained both by your deadlines and by the limits on the time that you have available for academic work.

To simplify matters, consider the case where you have two pieces of work – essays, let's say – to hand in: essay A in two weeks' time and essay B in three weeks' time. And let's assume you have two similar individual strategies – your time-demand charts have the same sequence of steps – but you haven't allocated any time to the various stages yet.

What are the possible overall strategies you could adopt? One possibility would be to spend the next two weeks working on essay A, hand it in, and then spend the next week working on essay B. What you would be doing here is forming an overall strategy by placing the two individual strategies end to end. By doing this you would actually be avoiding the issue of how to tackle the tasks simultaneously. But you would achieve this at the cost of limiting the time you spend on essay B to only one week.

Another possibility would be to start with whichever essay you feel most anxious about. This would certainly get you started but otherwise you aren't operating strategically, with the 'end points' of both essays in sight. And you probably wouldn't switch to the second essay until you became more anxious about that one, which could well be when time is getting short for it. So a 'responding to greatest anxiety' strategy has, paradoxically, the effect of generating anxiety rather than forestalling it. I don't think this strategy has a great deal to recommend it.

Yet another possibility would be to aim to split your time equally between the two essays, and to start by spending half a week on essay B. Although it may seem counterintuitive to start with the essay that has the furthest-away deadline, this would accomplish three things: it would allow you to check that you fully comprehend the task (topic) and to make enquiries if this turns out to be not straightforward; it would allow you to check on the availability of the books etc. that you would need and order them if they aren't to hand; and it would start you thinking about the essay B topic so that, even after you turn to essay A, the 'back of your mind' would be working subconsciously on essay B while the 'front of your mind' is working consciously on essay A. When you've completed essay A and handed it in, you would have a head start with essay B when you return to it. This 'interleaving' strategy must be worth a try, I think.

Essentially this overall strategy depends for its success on an important principle, namely that you have an individual strategy for each of your tasks

– that is, a clear view of the sequence of steps (events and stages) that must be gone through for each. This enables you to switch tasks at a clear point in a strategy – after a significant event, for example – rather than being rushed into switching when you're midway through a stage.

If you are tackling simultaneously a number of tasks of more than one kind, you can again use the interleaving strategy. If you are writing an essay (short term) and researching and writing a dissertation (long term) at the same time, your strategy could be to get the dissertation research under way, and then deal with and dispatch the essay before returning to the dissertation. If you are writing an essay that will be assessed and count towards your degree result and at the same time revising for unseen exams, you could divide your revision time into blocks – one for each of the exams you are taking – and write the essay in an interval between two of those blocks.

One-off tasks superimposed on your weekly routine

You will frequently have one-off tasks – with deadlines – imposed on your weekly routine. You will certainly appreciate having chunks of your 'own' time (see Chapter 8) to work on them. Consult your weekly super-timetable (see Chapter 4) to see where you can fit in their various stages. You may well need to adjust your super-timetable to achieve this. If this necessitates reducing the time you allow for sleep or recreation, do give yourself some 'recovery time' when you have completed your task and got it out of the way.

While you are working, notice when your energy flags, and give yourself a break as often as you need. Different people can work for different lengths of time without a break, so there is no rule to go by. Find out what suits you.

Chapter 10

Prioritize tasks... and make sure you don't overlook any

People often use the words 'priority' and 'prioritize' in connection with objectives, and rather loosely: 'My top priority is to get a good degree'; 'My first priority is to get this report finished.' (The words 'top' and 'first' add emphasis but, strictly speaking, they are redundant – both are implied by 'priority'.) And they often don't say what they are placing lower in the rank ordering that their prioritizing implies.

People assign priority to an objective on a variety of grounds. Thus they may assign objective A priority over objective B: (1) if objective A has the closer deadline, i.e. it has to be attained sooner; or (2) if the penalty for not attaining objective A by the deadline will be greater; or (3) if objective A is the one causing them more anxiety; and/or (4) if objective A is the one they see as requiring their effort here and now.

For the purpose of making best use of your time, I think the most useful of these definitions is number 4, as it provides a basis for action, for getting on with your work *now*. The fact that A's deadline is next month whereas B's deadline is the month after does not help you decide what to do today. Similarly the greater penalty attached to not attaining A, or the greater anxiety that A is causing you, doesn't help you decide what to do today, unless the deadline for both A and B is very imminent (like, tomorrow).

Let's get down to basics. The two objectives, A and B, both denote the completion of tasks; we can call those tasks A and B as well. In the here and now, you probably see the two tasks, A and B, as competing for your time, and you feel you have to take a decision as to which task you should give priority to, and accordingly work on. That decision has to be one for you alone – I can't help you with it – but it will be easier to take if you 'reframe' the choice in front of you.

To do this effectively you need to have an individual time-use strategy for each task and know where you have got to on each one. This simplifies your choice. You now have to judge whether your next task A stage should take priority over your next task B stage, or vice versa. You should find it easier to judge which of those two stages should take priority than to judge which *task* should take priority, since you're dealing in specifics and the likely consequences of each of the two alternatives will be clearer.

The message, then, is that rather than allocate your time on the basis of which *task* should take priority, you should allocate your time on the basis of which of the respective *stages* should take priority.

Be prepared for the results of this to be counterintuitive (not what you would expect) sometimes. Thus task A may have a closer deadline and carry a greater penalty for non-completion on time, but if you are on the verge of the 'sleep on it' stage for task A and the 'task comprehension' stage for task B, you will probably want to give priority to the latter, not the former.

To-do lists

A to-do list can be one of two things. It can be *either* a list of things that you intend to do, *or* it can be a list of things that you feel under pressure to do. It is a very good idea not to mix the two. Have two (or more) lists instead.

Start by drawing up a 'pressure list'. This might be painful, but it will be better to capture the pressures on paper rather than have them flitting around in your head. Make sure you have them all down. You will start to feel better when you begin crossing them off your list.

Now for your 'intention list'. (From now on I'll use the term 'to-do list' interchangeably with 'intention list'.) The purpose of this to-do list is to assist you in making best use of your time. So it should relate to the day or other 'time slot' ahead of you, and should be a list of those tasks and the particular stages of those tasks that you intend to work on during that time slot. Define those task stages as precisely as you can, so you are as clear as possible what it is that you are going to embark on.

In order for it to be helpful, a to-do list must be realistic. A realistic to-do list for a given time slot will contain only those task stages that you feel you can complete within that time slot. It follows that to construct a realistic to-do list you should have a realistic idea of the time each is likely to take, or the maximum time you will permit it to take. If you have not got realistic time estimates, or aren't prepared to set a deadline at the end of your time slot, you must be prepared to carry over unfinished stages to your next period of your own time.

To-do lists are ideal for showing your order of priority. (Don't confuse them with 'shopping lists', which don't.) At the top of the list will be 'must-do' task stages, ones that you feel absolutely *must* be completed within the time available to you. Below them will come those that you really do want to complete within the time slot, and next will come those that could, if you are pushed, be carried over.

Have several lists

You will almost certainly find that you need not one but several to-do lists. You should certainly have a to-do list for today and another one for 'By the end of the week'. You might want another one for 'Tomorrow' and possibly one for 'Next week'. A further one for 'By the end of term' might also come in handy – you can put all of this term's deadlines on it.

It will be a sensible practice to review your to-do lists every working day. In the evening (but not last thing – you don't want thoughts about work to be buzzing round in your head when you're trying to sleep), go over that day's list. Cross off those task stages that you have completed, and make a note of those you have to carry over to the next day. Now create the next day's list. Start with carried-over task stages, and add any new ones, including any that were already on your 'By the end of the week' list. Now arrange your next-day list in order of priority: first on the list will be the task stage you want to begin tomorrow's work session with.

If you find that you're using 'Next week' lists a lot, you might find it useful to print out a separate copy of your super-timetable for each week, and fit your 'Next week' list on to it.

While you're reviewing your to-do lists, notice how good – how realistic – your time estimates were. If you find you are consistently underestimating the time you will need for your task stages, then think about taking some action. There are three things you could do: (1) become more generous in your time estimates; (2) earmark an hour or so per day as a 'contingency allowance' to allow for overruns; or (3) look for ways of saving time on your task stages, e.g. by speeding up your work rate, or by identifying and cutting out less essential activities.

Chapter 11

Control the time you spend on a task

'Divergence' and 'convergence' modes

In the previous chapter, I focused on assessing the priority that a particular task and the associated task stages should have, and estimating the amount of time they will need. That is all part of planning. But once you actually get down to work, to *implementing* your plans, you are liable to find yourself impelled to do more – perhaps much more – than you had planned.

It is a characteristic of academic tasks – including individual task stages – that they will expand to fill the time available. There is always another book that you want to read or another journal article to look up, a related issue to explore, another problem or puzzle to solve, another test or trial run you could carry out. The source of these wants, or internal pressures, may be deep down in your subconscious: perhaps you feel impelled to do these things as 'displacement activities', to do them instead of moving forward towards completing your task.

If you give in to these internal pressures, you find your task expanding. You're in 'divergence mode'. You're working with more and more material; the scope of what you could put in your essay or report gets wider and wider; your 'field' gets broader and broader; your head is getting fuller and fuller of 'stuff'. You find it more and more difficult to move forward, and time becomes more and more pressing, especially when – as is invariably the case – there are several tasks competing for it.

How can you escape from divergence mode? The first thing you have to do is to monitor yourself, and in particular look out for the symptoms of being in that mode. These symptoms will include the following.

- Your physical activity: if you are doing more of what you have already done, like more reading and collecting more data, you are likely to be in divergence mode.

- Your intellectual activity: if you are trying to envisage your way forward, e.g. how you will approach your next task stage, but not succeeding, again you are likely to be in divergence mode.

- Your feelings: if you are feeling stuck, burdened, oppressed by your task – if your work has become a chore – once again you are likely to be in divergence mode.

If you are experiencing all of these symptoms simultaneously, you are certainly in divergence mode.

Escaping from divergence mode

If you have some or all of these symptoms, what can you do to escape from divergence mode and move forward? Here are some suggestions.

Physical activity

Stop what you have been doing – reading, collecting data, or whatever – and find something different to do connected with your task. It might help if you can find a different place to work. Sometimes just sitting in a different room, or even a different chair, will help to give you a different perspective.

So can taking some physical exercise, which will give your subconscious the chance to get to grips with your problem.

Intellectual activity

Think about the finished product that you're going to hand in. Focus on it; picture it in your mind's eye. Draw, or draw up, an outline of your product. If it's an essay or report, rough out your conclusions, however tentative they might be at this stage. Don't spend a lot of time on this: do it *quickly*! When you get back to your present task stage, you'll have a strong relevance test for everything you do: 'Will this contribute significantly to my conclusions?' When you apply this test, you'll find yourself in 'convergence mode': your field is narrowing rather than broadening.

An effective technique here is to get someone else to assist you. I have found that if I ask someone to tell me what their conclusions are going to be they can do so with remarkable fluency and cogency, to the point that I find myself saying repeatedly, 'Write that down!'

Feelings

The feeling that you want to get access to is *Urgency*! So remind yourself how close your deadline is. Look at your clock and calendar. Get out your 'By the end of the week' to-do list, divide the time you have available by the number of things you have to do, and give yourself a fright. This feeling should spur you towards finishing, and with a clearer idea of your finished product, you know what direction to be spurred in. You may be able to intensify your feeling of urgency by imagining that you're sitting an examination and have just an half an hour to go.

If this doesn't work it may simply be that your deadline isn't close enough. So why not switch to another task, or take the evening off?

Trying to do too much

One frequent cause of use-of-time problems is nothing more than trying to do too much, trying to fit in more reading, writing, calculating, practical work or whatever than the time you've allowed for it can accommodate. And perhaps as a result you never complete the task within the time allowed, so you miss the deadline for handing in, or you submit work that is rough and unpolished, if not actually incomplete, or you have to put off other tasks so you can finish this one.

Devoting one's effort to doing more of the same is a very 'static' and defensive way of behaving. It's a bit like holding on to the floor for security, and about as productive. Look for something different to do, some way of progressing. Having got to where you are now, be content with having done enough to get there, and think about where you could move on to. Where could you go to next in your thinking? How about rising above the floor, so you can see the big picture? How about looking for more economical ways of conveying ideas, more elegant ways of solving problems? This is not so much work as play. If you can hold back from trying to do too much, you'll have more time for play like this, and it will enrich your experience of being a student.

'Deadline rationing' and 'ring-fencing'

There are two other methods that you can use to limit the amount of time you spend on a task: 'deadline rationing' and 'ring-fencing'. To be effective, both require a certain degree of self-discipline and commitment.

Deadline rationing is also known as leaving things to the last minute. As the name implies, you can do this as a deliberate strategy rather than as a matter of carelessness. If you have an inflexible deadline to meet, not starting a task until late in the day automatically limits the amount of time you can spend on it. Self-discipline – or nerve – may be called for in delaying your start. But once you do start, you may find yourself energized by the impending deadline and the limited time available to you. This is a technique to be experimented with. It does not suit everybody.

A variant on deadline rationing is to set your own deadline. You need self-discipline to set a deadline and commitment in order to stick to it, and you can strengthen your commitment by making it known to your teachers and fellow students what you are doing; this gives you an added incentive to stick to it. Even though you have set your deadline yourself, it provides you with a 'finishing post' that – if you keep it in sight – focuses your attention and gets you converging before you have diverged too much.

Ring-fencing simply involves putting a 'ring', an inflexible boundary, round not only your time but other resources and material too. So you might say to yourself in a determined sort of way, 'I have enough books' or 'I have enough data', and in that way impose a limit on the scope and amount of work you do. With experience, this can be a very effective technique.

Chapter 12

Use your time productively

Students are often impressed – and sometimes depressed – by others who tell them how long they have spent working today or how many hours they have just spent in the library. What these paragons of virtue won't usually tell you, though, is how productive that time has been, how efficiently they have worked. Next time you are in the library, take a moment to look at the people around you. The chances are you'll see someone who is asleep, someone who is daydreaming, someone sending and receiving text messages, other people whose thoughts are pretty obviously elsewhere. They are in the library, certainly, but they are not using their time productively. So far as academic work is concerned, they are wasting time. So don't be taken in by accounts of hours spent 'in the library' or 'working'.

By the same token, there is little point in me telling you how many hours a week you ought to devote to academic work. You would accomplish more in five productive hours than in twenty not-very-productive ones. So let's address the question of productivity.

Think back to the last few full days (without teaching sessions or required attendance, or social activity), whether weekday or weekend, that your time was your 'own' and you decided to devote it to academic work. Are you satisfied with what you achieved on those days?

If you *are* satisfied with what you achieved, *and* if at some point during that day you experienced a sense of elation, a feeling that you 'had the bit between your teeth' and were achieving something worthwhile, congratulations! You're probably the best judge and quite possibly your harshest critic too. So I reckon you're doing well. If you're satisfied with what you achieved but didn't experience those other feelings, then there's a real possibility that you are being unjustifiably complacent.

If, on the other hand, you feel you might have made better use of the time on some occasions ... yes, there is always room for improvement. So what has been happening. Did you waste time? Did you not make best use of time because you were unclear as to what your task required of you? Were you prevented from concentrating on your task by stray thoughts or other distractions? Are you just a slow worker? Did you lack the books, equipment or other resources you needed? Was your physical or social environment, or just the time of day, not conducive to working? Let's take these possibilities one by one.

Time wasting

Some of the forms of time wasting are obvious. You are doing things other than working; sleeping, daydreaming, texting, chatting about non-work subjects come into this category. So does attending to interruptions during periods of time that you've designated for work. Here you are wasting time by throwing it away.

Time wasting also occurs when you are trying to work when you haven't got the necessary equipment. Examples are writing things out in longhand when your computer has crashed, and trying to piece together the argument in a book when you haven't got the actual book and have to rely on references to it in journal articles. Here you are wasting time by virtue of work taking longer than it should.

Doing unnecessary or irrational things wastes time. Sometimes you do such things because you can't think of anything better to do – for example, reading a whole book when the material you want is contained in just half a dozen pages; copying out by hand extracts from a book; repeating an activity over and over, and getting the same result each time – and sometimes you do them as a 'displacement activity', to put off something that you expect to find difficult or unpleasant. Working and reworking something to get it perfect becomes irrational after a couple of cycles; there is more on perfectionism in Chapter 14. You need to know when to settle for the less than perfect.

Question the value of activities that you take for granted. Note-taking from books and articles is one such activity. Every year in the run-up to exams I get students coming to me saying things like: 'I've got a stack of notes this high – what should I do with them?' And I have to say: 'I don't know.' Especially when you look at a publication for the first time, it's usually folly to start making notes, because you don't know what's relevant. Test this for yourself. If you're working on photocopies and underlining or using highlighter, how much do you underline or highlight? If the pages are covered in lines or a veritable rainbow of colour, you almost certainly don't know what material is relevant and so your work is largely unproductive and your time wasted. Don't open any publication without having some idea of what you're looking for; even if it's only the author's conclusions; scan it quickly for what you're looking for, and slap on a Post-it® note as a bookmark when you find something interesting. Make notes when you're on top of it and know what to make notes on. (See Chapter 3 for a little more on reading.)

If you're getting bogged down with a piece of work that just won't 'come right', perhaps you have (possibly unconsciously) been following a strategy of 'If at first you don't succeed, try, try again.' How about inventing an alternative strategy? Some of us find that 'If at first you don't succeed, try something different' works well. Remember, if something is a chore, there's almost certainly a better way of doing it.

Have you ever found yourself not knowing which of several tasks to work on, and ended up not working on any of them? Here you're wasting time through being indecisive. It's all too easy, when you don't know which of several tasks to work on, to end up not working on any of them. If you sense that this is happening to you, list them in order of priority and start working your way down the list.

Task comprehension

Have you ever felt while trying to work that you didn't really know what you were doing? Perhaps you found yourself doing things while having an uneasy feeling that they were not very relevant to the task in hand.

Especially if you are taking an essay-based subject, when you are set a task it may not be clear to you exactly what it is that you are expected to do. Now, it could be that working out what you are expected to do is part of the test – although you will be very fortunate if your teacher says as much to you. More likely, the topic or your instructions are badly worded, or you missed out on something that was said that would have made sense of it. There's a lot of room for misunderstanding here, as when your teacher issues you with a 'reading list' of monstrous proportions, which you think you have to wade through, and/or he or she says 'Read X, Y and Z' and you think you have to read the whole of each book instead of tracking down the relevant bits.

If you don't comprehend your task correctly, you are in trouble – and you certainly won't be making good use of your time. Just starting to write is almost certainly not the best way to go about your task. You'll be spending your time scratching your head, wondering what to do, instead of working. Or you'll be making incorrect assumptions about what you have to do, and setting off down the wrong road. Or, not knowing what's relevant, you'll try to write everything you know about the subject, in the hope that by doing so you'll manage to include what's wanted. You may work incredibly hard but your effort is unnecessary and misdirected – you're not making good use of your time and effort.

So think strategically. Work on interpreting the question (to clarify what you're expected to do), make a note of key terms that you need to look up, jot down notes for your introduction, and rough out a tentative structure for the essay or whatever you have to submit. This will give you a 'bird's-eye view' of the job in hand, will help you in searching out relevant extracts in your reading, and make it much easier to assemble your final product.

Accurate task comprehension is crucial to every time-use strategy. I can't emphasize this strongly enough. If the above suggestions don't help, you must ask your teacher. The fact that you have made an effort first should earn you some brownie points! Don't rely on what your fellow students say: they may have got it wrong. You need to have an authoritative statement.

Inability to concentrate

How good are your powers of concentration? Many students underestimate theirs, sometimes even coming to feel (quite wrongly, in my experience) that they have a congenital inability to concentrate. So let me ask you, was there any leisure activity in the last week or two that you spent a long time doing without losing concentration? Playing sport, computer games or a musical instrument, for example, or watching sport or a film, or reading novels. If you can answer this question with a 'Yes', there is probably nothing wrong with your powers of concentration. Certainly, if you are able to give your full attention to any of these for a sustained period, there is nothing congenital about your inability to concentrate on academic work.

So think about what happens when you try to work. Do you often/sometimes/never

- doze off or fall asleep?
- daydream, or simply find yourself thinking about non-work matters?
- allow other people to disturb you, rather than say 'I'm working: go away' (or, more politely, 'Please come back later')?
- engage in non-work 'displacement activities', like texting/telephoning/emailing, dropping work and going for coffee with friends, making a snack for yourself, doing housework?
- engage in 'pseudo-work' displacement activities, especially putting off handing in a piece of work so you can read one more book or article, or cover one more point, or revise what you've written one more time, or run one more check, or incorporate one more refinement in your practical work, when you really know that it is unnecessary to do so and you could perfectly well hand in your work immediately?

If your answer to all the above questions is 'never', then I congratulate you on having exceptional powers of concentration. You're a very rare case. Almost everyone has these experiences at some time or other, so here are some pointers to help you deal with them.

Dozing off

If you frequently doze off or fall asleep, then – unless you are sleep-deprived or suffering from over-indulging in alcohol – I suspect you are getting a certain message from your brain, a message that reads: 'Do not make me do this.' And at least part of the cause is likely to be something to do with the nature of your work and/or your approach to it. If the work involves computation, it could be tedious and repetitive, likely to bore anyone to tears. If the work involves reading, and your approach is to try to absorb great masses of stuff, that is something to which the human brain is not well suited, and which it literally finds a turn-off.

As ever, you need to develop an appropriate strategy. In the case of tedious computational work, this could mean breaking the work down into manageable chunks, so you spend only an hour or two at a time on it. In the case of reading, reframe your task. Think of it as a 'treasure hunt'. You are looking for those gems that you need for your essay or dissertation. Or think of what you are doing as detective work. We don't usually fall asleep when we are doing detective work: our brains are 'hooked' – engaged – by it.

Daydreaming

If you are finding yourself daydreaming or thinking about non-work matters, something is taking priority over your work. The 'something' could be a pressing issue, it could be that your work is currently tedious. Try taking a break from work and actually concentrating on that other matter for half an hour or an hour or so. Unless it has assumed the proportions of an obsession, in which case it could absorb all your time and then some, you may be able to get it out of the way, in which case it would be a good idea to do so. If it's the tedium of your work that is at the root of your distraction, look for ways of making it more interesting, or interleave it with another, more interesting task (see Chapter 9).

Disturbance by other people

Sometimes we welcome an interruption: it gives us an excuse to take a break from work. And if it's a friend that's doing the interrupting, it will probably be difficult to turn him or her away. But ask yourself if there might be other factors at work. Is your friend taking advantage of your good nature? Are you perhaps a bit afraid of losing their friendship if you don't give them your time when they want it? If you come up with the honest answer 'yes' to these two questions, I think you have to take a firmer line, and turn them away with a 'Please come back later.' A genuine friend will respect your need to concentrate when you're working.

Non-work 'displacement activity'

If you find yourself frequently engaging in non-work 'displacement activity', there is definitely some aspect of the relationship between you and your task that needs attending to. First, *be aware* that you are engaging in displacement activity. Then do try to get clear in your mind what the problem – the difficulty or dilemma – is. Are you afraid you haven't comprehended accurately what you are being asked to do? Is there a block that's stopping you from getting started? (See Chapter 13, on overcoming such blocks.) Did you get started OK but then come up against a block? Are you unable to decide which of two or more possible directions to go in?

An approach worth trying here is to write yourself a short note, a 'position paper', outlining your problem and the options open to you. This will help you to clarify the situation for yourself, and may clear the 'logjam', especially if you 'sleep on it' overnight. If this doesn't help, I suggest you talk to a sympathetic teacher or fellow student. Writing a position paper beforehand will help you to describe your problem clearly to them, and their input could be just what you need.

It could be, of course, that your excursion into displacement activity is prompted by simply feeling that you are thoroughly fed up with the whole thing. Sometimes just taking a break will reinvigorate you, especially if you use it to take some physical exercise. If you haven't time for that, try the interleaving strategy (again, see Chapter 9), switching to another task for a short time.

'Pseudo-work' displacement activities

If you have a pattern of 'pseudo-work' displacement activities, especially putting off handing in a piece of work, again there is something here that it would be a good idea to deal with. Not only are these activities taking up valuable time: the longer you put off handing in a piece of work, the more you are delaying starting on your next task. If you fear handing it in – if you're afraid that it will be criticized and perhaps that you will be humiliated by your teacher – you need to 'reframe' the experience, to see it in a different light. So regard handing in a piece of work as simply a means of eliciting feedback from your teacher. The test is not whether you have produced perfect work – the test is one for your teacher: is he or she capable of giving you useful feedback? See more on this in Chapter 14, on perfectionism.

The 'slow worker' syndrome

Students who feel they aren't being very productive often put it down to being 'slow': 'I'm a slow reader'; 'It takes me a long time to understand things'; 'I'm a slow writer.'

If you find yourself saying this sort of thing, ask yourself who or what you're comparing yourself to. Are you slow in relation to your own expectations? Are you slow in relation to other students? Such comparisons are frequently misleading.

So far as reading is concerned, whether of textbooks or topic-based books and articles, your expectations are probably not allowing for the fact that they are written in 'academic-speak', the specialist language of the subject. To all intents and purposes this is a foreign language to you. You would not expect to be able to pick up a book in a language that you don't have any knowledge of (Estonian? Farsi?) and be able to read and absorb the meaning of what is written in it, and nor should you if the language is academic-speak. As for comparisons with other students, you know perfectly well that some people have a gift for picking up foreign languages while others find them hard going; the same will be true of academic-speak, and you should not feel disheartened when you come across some of the gifted ones.

If you have experience of learning a foreign language, at school or subsequently, you may find that some of the techniques you used then can be applied to learning academic-speak. In particular, think about making a vocabulary book (dictionary) for yourself, with academic-speak terms translated into 'ordinary' English and accompanied by illustrations of how to use them. As with 'conventional' foreign languages, you can expect to build up fluency. When you started to learn Spanish (say), if someone asked you a question in Spanish you probably translated it into English, found the answer in English, and then translated the answer into Spanish. After a while, though, when someone asked you a question in Spanish you found yourself answering straight away in Spanish, without going through any intermediate steps. It is precisely that level of fluency that you need to have in the academic-speak of your subject(s). When you have attained it, you will be up to speed: you will no longer be a slow reader, and you will understand what you read.

If you feel you're a slow writer, there is almost certainly something you can do about this too. We use writing for two distinct purposes: to help us think, and to present our thoughts to an audience. If you try to do both at once, you'll be in trouble. You'll confuse yourself, you'll lose sight of what you're doing, the product will not be as good as it could be, and the process will take longer than it need do. Trying to do both at once is a recipe for slowness.

What to do instead? The first thinking you have to do is of course to get clear what your task entails. That done, brainstorm. Write down in note form, on paper or disk, the factual information you want to use, pertinent quotations that come to mind, your own ideas and thoughts. These notes are for your eyes only, and you should not at this stage be trying to edit or polish or refine them, let alone be thinking about how your audience will receive them. Now arrange your notes into a logical order: doing this will usually reveal some errors and omissions and stimulate some further ideas and things to say. Ideally your notes will be connected together in a chain of reasoning, which will automatically provide a 'flow' for the piece you are writing. These logically arranged notes of yours will serve as an outline for your piece, and now that you have this you can move into 'presentation mode': you can concentrate on editing and polishing and refining without having to revert to thinking the subject through.

Your physical and social environment, and the time of day

Days and time slots of a couple of hours or more when your time is your 'own' offer you a lot of scope for productive work, if you are able to make use of it. You can stay in your home or your room, you don't have to spend time travelling, you can have breaks whenever you want and you have the opportunity for a sustained, concentrated effort on a task. You should be able to choose furniture (especially seating), lighting, decor and background sound that suit you and help you work productively, and levels of heating and ventilation (fresh air is best) that you like. On the other hand, your physical and social environment may work against you. It may be irresistibly tempting to keep grabbing drinks and snacks, see what's on daytime TV, and generally potter about. And if there are other people around who don't respect your need to concentrate on work, you will certainly be better off elsewhere. Better to do the travelling and spend the day in the library, or a computing room, or even a café – somewhere where distractions are fewer and you can plan your day to suit yourself, dividing it up into chunks of time that you can manage comfortably.

Don't do all this on a day-to-day basis. Think strategically. Don't tackle each problem as it arises but put systematic defences in place. Establish routines. Make a point of spending the same time of the day or week regularly in the same place. If you have to work at home, 'ring-fence' your study time against interruption by telling all your family and friends that you have made it an inflexible rule that you are not available during those hours.

Finally, most of us find we work most productively at certain times of day. Be aware of your productive times, and make the most of them.

Chapter 13

Overcome blocks to getting started on a task

Would you say you are someone who habitually puts off doing things until the very last minute – or later? Procrastination, the phenomenon (some might call it an art!) of delaying doing something that you know you really ought to be getting on with, is for many people a common feature of their working life. As a student, you'd be extremely unusual if you have never engaged in it.

A very common form of block to getting started is the one known as 'writer's block'. If you're always putting off writing tasks, or you just sit and chew your pen or stare at the screen for hours without inscribing anything, while your thoughts go round in circles, that could be what you've got. But in quantitative subjects too you may find yourself in the same position if you're faced with a problem that seems intractable. And the consequence is, of course, that you aren't making good use – or, indeed, any use – of the time you spend in this state of suspended activity.

It could be, I suppose, that there is something in your personal psychological make-up that predisposes you to seize up when faced with a demanding task, but it is not within the scope of this book to deal with matters of psychology. What I can say, though, is that in my experience students often get 'blocked' simply because they are lacking in one or both of the two elements of task comprehension, namely (1) knowledge of what they are expected to produce, and (2) knowledge of how to proceed, of what to do to get started. Here are some strategies that should help.

Be clear what you are expected to produce

In essay-based subjects, lack of clarity as to what you are expected to produce often comes about because you have been given a subject but not a question or a proposition, so your task is not specific enough to provide guidance about the product. A question manifestly calls for an answer, so you know your teacher will want to see your answer and the chain of reasoning by which you arrived at it. A proposition is a question in disguise – the question being 'Do you agree with the proposition?' – and requires to be taken apart and to have its elements carefully scrutinized. A subject on its own, however, gives you no clues about what is required.

So if you are set nothing more than a subject, the first thing you should do to get started is to look for interesting questions to ask about it. One or two will usually be enough. Then think about how you are going to reason your way from question to answer: this will give you a structure for your essay. Whatever you do, don't get sucked into an open-ended activity, like reading without looking for something specific. You could read and read for days on end, and perhaps build up a huge stack of notes, and then still find you don't know how to start creating your essay. So don't go down that road.

Your teachers also have ways of confusing you about what you are expected to produce. They may set you a topic like this: 'What are the causes of social exclusion? Discuss with reference to inner cities.' What are you meant to do? Are you meant to answer the question, showing the reader how you identify the causes and the way in which, under certain circumstances, they combine to produce 'social exclusion'? Or are you meant to *discuss* the causes, which could be interpreted as no more than 'write down some interesting things about them'?

Teachers in some disciplines have their own special refinements when it comes to confusing students. For example, teachers in essay-based subjects commonly ask perverse questions beginning 'Discuss the extent to which you agree that . . .' – perverse, and hence confusing, because what they really want you to discuss is the substantive proposition, not the extent to which you agree with it.

Similarly, some teachers in essay-based subjects will confuse you by asking you a question and then telling you: 'I want to see a clear argument' or 'You will be marked on the strength of your argument.' Please, please, observe that *an argument is not an answer to a question*. A question should set you off on a chain of reasoning, a path of marshalling relevant evidence and drawing reasoned conclusions from it. But being asked for an argument will tempt you into responding to the question with an assertion, usually followed by a miscellany of points to back it up; your chain of reasoning is lost. I suggest that when you are asked for an argument you interpret this as a request for *reasoning*; you should be on safe ground, so long as your reasoning is sound, and you won't be diverted from your path to your answer.

Here's another example of instructions that confuse. Law students have for years and years been faced with two distinct categories of assignment: essay questions and problem questions. Essay questions could be identified by the instruction 'Discuss' and problem questions by the instruction 'Advise', as in 'Advise Fred' or 'Advise Mary'. In recent years more and more students have reported being confused by questions setting out a problem 'scenario' but giving instructions along the lines of 'Discuss the remedies available to X'; the implication here is that they should answer the problem question by writing an essay. If you find yourself on the receiving end of such questions, you *must* ask your teacher exactly what it is that he or she expects from you.

Have a strategy for getting started

If you don't have a strategy for getting started, the likelihood is that you will put off getting started as long as you can, and that when you do get started you will do something silly, like – if you have to write an essay – trying to put perfectly formed sentences on to the page from the very start. This will quickly get you very frustrated, because you are trying to do two incompatible things simultaneously: you're trying to brainstorm and to edit at the same time.

If you find yourself blocked when you are faced with a problem to solve or some other kind of task to carry out, there are three strategies you could use to overcome the block:

1. The heuristic strategy, where you ask questions about the task
2. Identifying what it is that your teacher wants and will reward you for, and
3. Formulating your own systematic approach.

Let's look at each of these in turn.

The heuristic strategy

With an heuristic strategy, here are some questions you might usefully ask:

- Does this task or problem fall into a category that I recognize, that I can put a name to? If your answer is 'yes', then you already have some familiarity with it and should be able to build on this.

- Is this task or problem similar to others that I've undertaken or solved in the past? If so, techniques that you have used in the past should be applicable here, especially if there is some fundamental principle underlying new and old.

- What information do I need in order to be able to undertake this task or solve this problem? If you can identify your information needs, you can then go on to track down this information.

- Can I represent this problem differently, e.g. by translating it into another language? In economics and quantitative subjects, translating a problem from words or tables into graphs or equations is precisely what is needed.

- Can I assume that the problem is actually capable of being solved, or has an unique solution? Sometimes this piece of information will be what you need to open up a way forward.

- What if …? Asking questions of the kind, 'What if it were true?' or 'What if such-and-such a variable had such-and-such a value?' can sometimes help you 'unlock' a proposition or problem. If you're at your wits' end, it's always worth playing or juggling with a problem: turn it inside out or upside down to get a different perspective on it.

Identifying what your teacher wants and will reward you for

The strategy here is, in essence, to get inside your teacher's head – to see the subject in the same way that he or she does. Here are some examples.

- If your teacher sees the subject as defined by writings, the first thing you should do when issued with a new essay topic is to ask yourself: 'What has been written about it – in particular, what has been written about it recently?' If the writings are heavily theoretical, ask yourself what theory the topic relates to.

- If your teacher sees the subject as a debating ground, your starting point when faced with a new essay topic should be to ask yourself: 'What is the debate that this topic relates to?' If the debate focuses on topical issues, your starting point should be 'What's new here?'

- If your teacher sees the subject as a collection of practical techniques, when faced with a new problem you should lose no time in asking: 'What technique(s) am I meant to apply?'

Identifying how your teacher sees his or her subject calls for careful observation on your part. Read anything that he or she has written. Notice how they construct their lectures: as a string of quotations from published writings; as a debate where you have to choose whose side you're on; as a demonstration of how to apply practical techniques. Just as when someone (especially someone in authority) asks you a question it is sensible to reply in the same language that they use, it is sensible to reply using their 'mindset'.

If you are fortunate, you will get some help from the feedback that you're given on your work. Not all feedback is useful: comments like the succinct 'A-, very good' and the patronizing and uninformative 'Your structure lets you down' get you nowhere on their own. Make a point of asking: 'What could I have done to gain a better mark?' This question is often effective at eliciting an insight into a teacher's mindset.

If you are taking a problem-centred subject, the teaching you receive may take the form of setting you problems for 'homework' followed by classes in which the correct solutions are demonstrated. These classes are liable to be less helpful than they could be, because the teacher goes straight in to applying the technique but does not demonstrate the thinking that goes into appreciating the problem: identifying the *kind* of problem that it is and the appropriate technique for solving it. Moreover, your teacher is likely to have some talent for the subject and an intuitive grasp of it, and a corresponding inability to put himself or herself in the position of a student new to the subject.

To bridge this gap between you and your teachers, try to get some one-to-one time with them, and instead of them doing the demonstrating, *you* demonstrate to *them* how *you* are trying to appreciate the problem. This should give them some sense of where you are 'coming from', and enable them to put you right by modifying your appreciation of the problem, rather than simply telling you that what you are doing is wrong and showing you something different.

Formulating your own systematic approach

This works best for essay-based subjects. First of all, consider the task in front of you. Before you can produce an essay, or indeed a dissertation or a piece of writing for publication, you have to do some thinking. It is the experience of many academics – probably the great majority, I suspect – that writing plays an important part in their thinking process. This 'early stage' writing does not consist of producing perfectly formed sentences – it consists of 'rough work', making notes. These notes are for the writer's eyes alone. It's only in the later stages of editing and producing a final draft that the writer thinks about presentation, crafting the piece to appeal to the reader. This is a good scheme for you to follow.

The question 'How do I get started?' is thus replaced by another: 'How do I make useful notes that will aid my thinking?' Here is a formula for doing this, a formula for 'structured brainstorming', which I have seen many students follow, with remarkably good results. It starts from the premise that you have been assigned a topic for your essay. The formula involves thinking about, and making rough notes on

- background/overview/context
- interpretation, of the topic and the individual words and phrases that

comprise it (including any instruction, such as 'Discuss' and 'Critically evaluate ...')

● methodology, the reasoning you will employ

● materials, the documentary and other sources you will use.

Background/overview/context
Ask yourself the following questions. Why is this subject interesting? Does it relate to a current debate among academics or to a topical issue? Is there a 'big picture' that it fits into? (If you subsequently begin your essay with this, your teachers will usually be impressed to see that you are aware of it and have given thought to it.)

Interpretation
It is absolutely crucial that (a) you ask what *meanings* you should assign to each of the individual words and phrases that make up the topic, and (b) that you look for and *challenge* any wording that has an 'underlying message', a statement or instruction that is implicit – 'sneaked in', so to speak – rather than made explicit.

Under 'meanings', look out in particular for

● words that different writers use to mean different things (it will be sensible to show your reader that you are aware of these different usages rather than opting for just one without saying why you are doing that)

● abstract and technical terms – these may need translating

● colloquial – 'ordinary' – language and figures of speech, such as metaphors; these certainly will need translating, into more precise terms.

Underlying messages that you should identify and challenge will include the following:

● Presumptions – for example, the presumption that something exists (a purported fact) or is 'a good thing'.

● Generalizations: these are a form of presumption but worth distinguishing as a separate category. For example, if you are asked 'Why did Latin America default on its debts in the 1930s?', you should notice the presumption, the underlying message, that Latin America can be treated as a monolithic whole. You aren't explicitly being asked to challenge this, but you must do so if you are to get a good mark; you must distinguish between the different countries (or some of them) that comprise Latin America, because each has its own particular record of treatment of its debts in that period.

- Words that include or exclude or quantify: these too may need to be challenged. If little words like 'all' or 'only' appear in the topic, to get good marks your essay may need to show that the topic is true of 'some', or 'others', or is true under some circumstances but not others.

- Time-related words and expressions: these may specify dates, time spans, frequencies, and so on. For example 'has/have been', 'has/have/will become', 'today', 'currently', 'still', 'rarely', 'sometimes', 'frequently', 'often', 'always'. Or they may specify time-related processes, such as 'development', 'evolution', and sequences and successions of events or situations.

- Wording that conveys a claim, assertion, judgement, opinion or an assumption of some kind. You should bring these out – make them explicit – if they are hidden, and always test or challenge them.

- Wording that denotes cause and effect, like 'was significant', 'was responsible for', 'could not have taken place without'. It will usually be a good idea to cover in your essay some or all of the following: other possible causal factors, mechanisms and processes that could have operated, surrounding circumstances and conditions, and 'counterfactuals', alternative (imagined) effects that might have come about but did not.

- Wording that – usually misleadingly – conveys degree or distance, such as 'How far . . .?' and 'To what extent . . .?' If you're asked in a cause-and-effect question 'How far/to what extent was X responsible for . . .?', you should interpret this as a question about X *in relation to other factors*, so your essay must deal with these other factors as well as X.

Methodology

Most essay topics come in one of two forms: a question, which you are required to answer, or a statement (proposition), which you are required to discuss or comment on. Virtually all statements can be expressed as – turned into – questions, either by altering the wording slightly or prefixing it with the words 'Is it valid to say that . . .' and tacking a question mark on the end. Your methodology is your way of getting from that question to your answer: the method(s) and/or principles that you will use. Of course, you 'get' from question to answer by a process of reasoning, so your methodology is in effect a toolkit for reasoning. A good essay will set out the reasoning by which you have got from question to answer, so it will take the reader along that same path. (If you're studying any subjects that involve solving problems, you should be familiar with this process: it's analogous to the process by which you get from problem to solution.)

If all this sounds a bit abstract, here's how to make it concrete. First, express your essay topic as a question, if it isn't in that form already. (Never, ever, set out merely to 'write about X' or to 'look at Y'.) Once you have that question, ask yourself another: 'How can I tell (discover, find out) what the answer is? When you have your answer to this second question, you have identified your methodology.

Most methodologies take the form of a sequence of steps. Typically the first step will be to elaborate on the subject: you say more about it, identify its significant features, or whatever. Your next step might be to analyse it, or 'compare and contrast' it with something else, extrapolate trends, offer alternative views of it: whatever is appropriate. If that step generates 'findings' of some kind, you can then go on to the next, which would be to comment on the significance of those findings. The range of possibilities is great, so it's difficult and not very helpful to try to go further and offer a more detailed 'recipe'. But if you have never before thought about methodology when writing an essay, try it now; by focusing your mind on things you can actively do, it offers you a way of getting past writer's block.

Materials

All academic writing involves making use of documentary and other materials. These may be publications drawn from the academic literature, or from the professional literature if there is one. You may be using formal publications (e.g. statutes and law reports) and/or official and other data sources (e.g. census reports). Depending on your subject, you may get information through other communication channels too. There's no need to make heavy weather of this: my point is simply that you will usually find it useful to think in advance about the materials you'll be using. It will prompt you to check whether there is anything you've left out and whether you are making sufficient use of the academic literature to satisfy your teachers. Remember that one of the things teachers look for when reading your essays is evidence that you have read widely – and, of course, thought about what you have read.

Conclusion

A good way of getting started on an essay – and getting past any block you might have come up against – is to make rough notes on background, overview, context; interpretation; methodology; and materials. And here's an added bonus: when you've got those notes, boil them down into three or four sentences; now add another, beginning 'In this essay I shall …' and outlining the series of steps your methodology will take you through. Hey presto! You now have the Introduction to your essay. It really is as straightforward as that.

Chapter 14

Stop being such a perfectionist

A perfectionist is someone for whom work that is not perfect is not acceptable. Perfectionism gets a bad press these days, and it is self-evidently true that when it comes to making best use of time, perfectionists are at a disadvantage. It takes them longer to produce a piece of work, and they are often inhibited from handing in work on time because they fear it isn't good enough.

In the academic world, however, there is something to be said for perfectionism. Perfectionists take care over their work. They are meticulous. They examine evidence carefully, they are cautious in drawing inferences from it, and they take the trouble to check their calculations and their reasoning scrupulously. So don't let anyone persuade you that perfectionism is necessarily a bad thing.

Because perfectionism has its advantages, I have deliberately not entitled this chapter 'Stop being a perfectionist'. The title that I have chosen – 'Stop being *such* a perfectionist' – is intended to convey the message that you should not take perfectionism to extremes. It is important to have a sense of proportion, to accept and be comfortable with applying the criterion of 'good enough' to your work.

Perfectionism is a trait that is less easy to detect in oneself than you might think. While one of the commonly accepted indicators is a reluctance to hand in work – we tell ourselves and anyone who asks, 'There's more that I need to do on it' – it could be that we started too late and haven't finished, or that there are mysterious psychological factors at work. Some people find it difficult to 'let go' of a piece of work, some are inhibited by the fact that their work will be exposed to the critical and perhaps unsympathetic gaze of another person. These various factors aren't mutually exclusive, of course: many people who aim at perfection also find it difficult to let go and become anxious at the prospect of exposing their work to others.

Even if these other factors aren't present, the true perfectionist has a hard time of it. Forever seeking after perfection is liable to be enormously time-consuming. And in some subjects, especially essay-based ones where there is no right answer to a question, perfection is impossible to attain. If the other factors are present, being a perfectionist as well can make life quite a misery.

May I ask you a few diagnostic questions? Think about your recent experience and try to answer them with 'Yes, many', 'Yes, a few' or 'No'.

- Have there been occasions when you've handed in work that you're not satisfied with?

- Have there been occasions when you've said to yourself 'I must just read one more article/one more book before handing in my essay'?

- Have there been occasions when you've 'tinkered' with your work, spending hours and hours going over it but ending up by making only small changes?

- Have there been occasions when you have found it difficult to 'let go' of a piece of work?

- Have there been occasions when you've felt anxious at the prospect of exposing your work to other people?

Unless you come up with five straight 'No' answers, there is certainly something you can do to make life easier for yourself and, at the same time, reduce significantly the hours you spend on every piece of work you hand in for marking. The principle here is 'reframing', learning to see and experience your situation in a different way. For example, at present you may – deep down – feel that handing in work to be marked amounts to submitting yourself to a test in which you can't do well, or feel that it's like entering a race you can't win. If you ever had a bad experience as a child with a teacher who ridiculed your work or humiliated you in front of other children – perhaps you produced something that you were proud of only to be slapped down and have it rubbished and laughed at – that experience can come back to haunt you later on: consciously or subconsciously you recall painful memories of it. Here you are, trying to do something worthwhile, and you are being reminded that again you will have to expose it to your teachers, who will certainly not have been appointed to their posts on the basis of their social skills or ability to empathize with learners.

Reframing will involve accustoming yourself to regard handing in a piece of work in a completely different way. Instead of thinking about it as a public test or trial, think about it as a means of getting feedback from your teacher – of discovering what he or she wants from you, and of getting a clearer idea of what their expectations of you are and what you could do to improve the standard of your work. Feedback! Feedback!! Feedback!!! Even if the comments you get at first are not constructive, once the principle that you will receive comments is established, you are in a position to go back for more and ask how your work could be improved. Unhelpful comments, like insensitive remarks in front of other people, indicate that it's your teacher, not you, who has a problem. It's their problem! Remember that.

If your course is an essay-based one, you may also be able to reframe your perception of the writing task. It could be that you see writing as getting perfectly formed sentences down on the page. If so, you are trying to do two very different things at once, namely brainstorm and edit for presentation. A bit of you is trying to produce creative work, and at the same time another bit of you – the editor – is sitting on your shoulder telling you that you need to be clearer or more concise or rigorous or whatever. This is a recipe for confusion and for producing an incoherent mess.

Escape this situation by reframing your perception of the writing task. Instead of thinking of writing as a single, unitary task, think of it as a task made up of two distinct and intellectually very different activities: brainstorming for ideas is one and editing for presentation is the other. Brainstorming comes first. Brainstorming should be uninhibited and freewheeling, however untidy and undisciplined it is. Get those ideas out in the open. Make rough notes, for your eyes only. You might like to follow the suggestions I made in the previous chapter, under 'Formulating your own systematic approach'.

If your on-the-shoulder editor tries to interrupt you while you are brainstorming, tell him or her to shut up and go away. They will have their chance later. Imagine them slinking away into another room or out of the building altogether.

Once you have a collection of rough notes – here's a good tip – don't try to force them into a mould of some kind but see if there's some underlying pattern you can bring out, a logical order waiting to be elicited, a structure waiting to be found. (There usually is one.) This is a task that your 'brainstormer' and 'editor' can cooperate in, so give it a go. When you have found it, your editor can get down to the task of refining your ideas into polished English prose.

Chapter 15

Make sure you meet a deadline

Make a start as soon as possible

Paradoxical though it may seem, the first rule of meeting deadlines is to do with making a start. Whether you've got six months or six days until your deadline, make a start as soon as possible. Do this however remote the deadline may feel at the moment. Deadlines have a habit of creeping up on you. Plant the seed at the back of your mind.

Equip yourself with a notebook or folder (plastic, card or electronic). Think about your topic and ways of approaching it, and write down your thoughts. Brainstorm and write down the ideas that occur to you. Make a list of possible sources: books, articles, websites, people to talk to . . . Attend any workshops that are organized for you.

But don't wait for other people to do things: take the initiative.

If you have a choice of topics, and reckon you have enough time, don't feel obliged to choose between them just yet. Make a list of them, and write down the pros and cons of each as they occur to you. Try to get the feel of what it would be like to live with each one, and whether you would be comfortable with it.

When you have some spare time or want a break from other things, track down publications and do some looking up. When you find potentially useful material, make photocopies of pages from articles and books.

You're in 'divergence mode' at the beginning. How long you stay in it will depend on how long you stay feeling comfortable with it – you don't feel things are getting out of hand – and how close your deadline is.

As you get into it, and once you have settled on your topic and how you are going to approach it, draw up a time-use strategy showing the various stages that you anticipate going through (see Chapter 3).

The middle period

The middle period of work towards a deadline – whether it be two months or two days – is usually a time before anxiety kicks in or ratchets up to a fierce level. By the end of this period you need to have moved from divergence mode to convergence mode. You need to be able to see where your work is heading and to have an idea of what the finished product will look like. Thus you need to have an outline – a structure – in your mind for your essay, write-up, report, dissertation or whatever. This will help you in two ways. It will enable you to sort through your materials according to relevance, so you can discard those that you won't be needing any more. And it will allow you to move on from 'writing as thinking' to 'writing for presentation' – the 'assembly job' of putting your finished product together.

Approaching the deadline

As the deadline approaches, you're conscious of running out of time, and stress builds up. A certain amount of stress is not necessarily a bad thing – it will keep you awake and give you energy. But you need to know what to do with this energy, and you need to maximize the amount of time you have available to complete your work.

What to do with your energy

It's when you don't know what to do with your energy that panic sets in. Panic stops you working rather than helps you; people don't work smoothly or take sensible decisions when they're panicking. So being able to channel your energy is crucially important. Here are some suggestions.

Visualize your completed product. Pay particular attention to your conclusions. If you're not yet certain what these are going to be, make rough notes, put these into some kind of order, then knock them into shape. Aim to do this *quickly*, in an hour or two, no longer. You can polish them up later. It's much, much easier to write when you know what conclusions you're heading towards than when you're writing in an 'open-ended' way, heading towards the unknown. (It's the difference between painting by numbers, when everything is mapped out for you and you're just following instructions, and painting when you're still deciding what to put where in your composition.)

Break down the work that still remains to be done into separate chunks – for example, 'Write section on methods', 'Add statistical appendix', 'Compile list of references' – and make a list of these. For each, make an estimate of the minimum time it will take, and write that in on your list. Now check the list against the time you have left (see below). If there's no way you can get everything in, look for items you can leave out or cut down. Tackle the shortest or easiest first; you may find it takes you less time than you anticipated.

Maximizing your available time

You can maximize the time you have available by minimizing the time available for other activities. So clear the decks: put off everything you possibly can, everything that doesn't have a higher priority than your deadline task. Postpone social events. At a pinch you can probably miss a week's worth of lectures and classes (not recommended, but it's not the end of the world if you do).

How much sleep do you need? When you're working flat out you can probably get by with two hours less than normal, but try to gain these by setting your alarm clock and getting up earlier in the morning (and having a decent breakfast) than by going to bed later. If you stay up working into the early hours, the risk is that you'll oversleep the next day and create more and more disruption to your work/sleep pattern. If you've tried this before, you'll know how well you cope with working late. If you think you'll have to be working all through the night at some point, make it the last night before hand-in, that way you won't have to deal with the after-effects until your work is out of the way.

Finally, avoid alcohol and an excess of coffee and other stimulants, but do feed yourself properly. This is not a time to be dieting and, in my experience, if you eat properly a loss of sleep can be easier to bear.

Chapter 16

Catch up when you're lost time

The weekly cycle of academic work grinds remorselessly on during term time, paying no heed to your state of health, clashes of deadlines and any difficulties you may have mastering the work itself. Inevitably, students fall behind. Hardly anybody doesn't fall behind at some point. The question then arises of how to catch up.

It's a different issue in term time from vacation. If you're on the weekly 'treadmill', making time to catch up on one of your courses must mean losing time elsewhere, on that course or others.

A common formulation of the problem is 'Should I concentrate now on catching up what I missed, or should I aim to keep up with the course so I don't fall behind any further and hope to make what I've missed later?' My answer is usually that it will depend on the kind of course that it is; in particular, whether (a) it is a course that 'builds' from week to week, so that in any week you need to be familiar with what has gone before to make sense of the proceedings; or (b) it is a course that is divided into self-contained chunks that can be taken in pretty much any order. If the latter, keeping up with the course for now and filling in the missing bits later will be the best strategy.

If the course is one that builds, though, you do need to fill in the missing bits. Here are a few suggestions.

- As far as you can, clear your schedule for a week of everything that isn't essential. Put off everything that can be put off. Skimp on everything else. Make a concentrated effort to catch up, using all the resources you've got: lecture handouts and notes (borrow other people's), textbooks and other *essential* reading matter, and past exam papers.

- It is quite likely that not all missing bits will be equally crucial. So identify those that are crucial; ask your fellow students and (unless you feel it would be tactless) your teachers for some guidance about this. Then clear your schedule as above and give yourself a crash course in the crucial bits.

- Don't labour over anything. If you find you're stuck or held up somewhere, make a note of the problem and press on. By doing this you can isolate the problem: viewed from 'the far side' it can often be seen to be less of an obstacle than it seemed at first. Having identified the problem, again seek help with it. It is particularly important when you're racing against the clock/calendar that you keep up the momentum and don't let problems become obsessions and that you don't get into 'bashing your head against a brick wall' mode. Sleeping on a problem and letting your subconscious get to grips with it may also produce a dividend: it's worth giving it a try.

During vacation you are under much less pressure, but it's still worth thinking in terms of giving yourself a crash course. Otherwise your catch-up task may well expand to fill the time available. And time taken catching up with the past is time not available for moving forward.

Chapter 17

Monitor and review

Approaches to monitoring and reviewing

You will find it extraordinarily useful as a student if you can develop the knack of monitoring and reviewing your activities and your progress, and adjusting your strategies and technique accordingly. There are many different approaches you can take:

- Assessing how well you coped with a situation
- Comparing your objectives to your actual attainments
- Making before and after comparisons of how you feel
- Keeping a log
- Taking a detached view of yourself.

Let's look at each of these in turn.

Assessing how well you coped with a situation

In your mind's eye, 'revisit' a situation – when you were faced with a difficult task or choice to make, perhaps – and ask yourself how well you coped. Don't do this immediately afterwards – wait until you are cool and calm and can view the situation dispassionately. Ask yourself whether you might have benefited by dealing with the situation differently.

Comparing your objectives to your actual attainments

If it turned out that you didn't attain your objective, give yourself a few days to get over it, then ask yourself what went wrong. You may get some useful feedback if you ask your teacher. Ask the additional question: 'What could and should I have done to get a better result?'

Making before and after comparisons of how you feel

This can be a valuable technique for realizing how much progress you've made, and – if you find you're feeling much more on top of one of your subjects, say – giving you a great boost in confidence.

Keeping a log

Just observing how you have been spending your time can be a valuable activity. If you feel you may have been wasting time, a log like this can be valuable in showing you where the time went.

Taking a detached view of yourself

You can get useful insights into how you have been approaching your work, and into what you have been doing with your time, by imagining that you are outside the window of your room or workplace looking in at yourself. Or imagine that you are sitting in one of the back-row seats of a cinema watching a film of yourself at work. It may be difficult to get the hang of this at first, but it is worth persevering with. This technique can be applied in conjunction with the others, and you may find it useful to do this.

▼ ▼ ▼

Whatever techniques you do apply, do your best to get into the self-appraisal habit. It will stand you in good stead both in your student career and in the rest of your life.

Queries, feedback, updates, web links

If you have any queries about making best use of your time that this book hasn't covered, or any suggestions for improving the book, please log on to my personal website

www.student-friendly-guides.com

and send me an email. I'll be glad to answer any queries, and all suggestions for improvements will be very gratefully received.

And don't forget to check out the website regularly for updates to this and other Student-Friendly Guides, and for useful web links.